ALSO BY ELSPETH BARKER

O Caledonia: A Novel

Dog Days: Selected Writings

NOTES

FROM THE

HENHOUSE

ON MARRYING A POET,

RAISING CHILDREN AND CHICKENS,

AND WRITING

ELSPETH BARKER

With an introduction by Raffaella Barker

SCRIBNER

New York   London   Toronto   Sydney   New Delhi

Scribner
An Imprint of Simon & Schuster, LLC
1230 Avenue of the Americas
New York, NY 10020

Copyright © 2023 by The Estate of Elspeth Barker
Introduction copyright © 2023 by Raffaella Barker
Originally published in Great Britain in 2023 by Weidenfeld & Nicolson

First Scribner trade edition March 2024

SCRIBNER and design are registered trademarks of Simon & Schuster, LLC.

Simon & Schuster: Celebrating 100 Years of Publishing in 2024

For information about special discounts for bulk purchases, please contact
Simon & Schuster Special Sales at 1-866-506-1949 or business@simonandschuster.com.

The Simon & Schuster Speakers Bureau can bring authors to your live event.
For more information or to book an event, contact the Simon & Schuster Speakers Bureau at
1-866-248-3049 or visit our website at www.simonspeakers.com.

Interior design by Jaime Putorti

Manufactured in the United States of America

10 9 8 7 6 5 4 3 2 1

Library of Congress Cataloging-in-Publication Data has been applied for.

ISBN 978-1-6680-2215-3
ISBN 978-1-6680-2216-0 (ebook)

"There is no reciprocity; men love women, women love children, children love hamsters."

—ALICE THOMAS ELLIS

CONTENTS

CONTENTS

PART 3—WIDOWHOOD

PART 4—NEW CHAPTER OF LIFE

MISCELLANY

LIFE'S MOTORWAY

We have a family photograph, taken in the shed where the tractors lived during my childhood and where, eventually, my father's
mouldering Mercedes, a skeleton of a canoe, and a Sinclair C5 car
would all be laid to rest. The photograph was taken in the early
1970s, on a rainy day when a journalist and a photographer from
The Sunday Times came to see my father the poet and his family.
We all assembled in the broken-down cart shed. The kind of place
photographers favour. My father, George, his waterproof jacket
zipped, holds my hand, grinning out into the dripping October day.
I hide inside my new hooded school coat, shy at seven. My brothers,
one defiant in his cowboy hat, the other with a baseball cap askew
over his ear, are in front of us. My mother, Elspeth, stands forward,
rain beads in her hair, marshalling our donkeys, who had wandered in to see what the fuss was about. Elspeth's gaze sparkles,
her beauty radiates, wellies muddy, mackintosh buttoned, hands
lost in the manes of the donkeys. She is as poised and self-possessed

as if she were being photographed in Cecil Beaton's studio, and her presence is arresting. We are grouped like a family of statues, yet the drip of rain through the leaking roof, the animals' implacable disapproval, and the escape we three children are itching to get on with are palpable as we face the lens, our expressions lit with the electricity of connection to one another. A family. And then, behind my father, something seems to move in the captured stillness of the photograph. Out of the darkness a face appears. A profile, light glancing off cheekbone. Eyes down, a brow carved, nose aquiline, the mouth curved beneath in symmetrical beauty. Who can it be? How can it be? No one else was there that day. No one can make sense of it. Not now, not ever in the many years the picture hung in the kitchen of my mother's house. The photographer was interrogated, the barn was investigated. Nothing. A ghost. An angel. Why not? No other explanation seemed possible and, faced with the evidence, it was reasonable. In our world anyway.

Sorting out my mother's papers, after her death, I came across the photograph again, its mystery still unsolved. No answers likely, as, counting the ghost, three of its subjects were now dead. And then, while reading my mother's essays for this collection, I found her words:

> The ancient Greeks had a notion that the image lay waiting to be discovered and released. So, it seems to me, that images deliberately lurk about in the effluvium of our lives until such time as we recognise them. They have always been there waiting for this moment.

Her musings on the significance of an image are as real and apposite to the moment as if she were talking directly to me. This is the case with so much of what she writes. Every story flies through the years to land in the moment it seems it was made for. And that, perhaps, is the hallmark of great writing. It also makes sense of the angel.

This book, created from an excavation of Elspeth's essays and short stories, also seems to have flown through the years to land here and now. The pieces we have brought to light were originally published some years ago, the essays alongside her journalism in a volume, *Dog Days*, and the short stories accompanying a 2010 reissue of *O Caledonia*. Working with a small publishing house, Black Dog Books, my mother had, with some diffidence, put together fragments and thoughts that marked the elements of life that compelled her imagination and her art. Reading them now, when it is no longer possible to talk to her, I am struck by both the immediacy of her voice and the enduring romance of her spirit. Some of the essays are straightforward autobiography, others are written as short stories, but the material explored comes from her own experience and, as such, lands vivid and alive in the reader's mind. If *O Caledonia* was a version of Elspeth's childhood in her own words, it made sense to find a way for her to continue to tell her story. For me to weave the essays and stories into a loose chronology, leaving a handful of pieces to make up an appendix, was an experience as close as mortality allows to talking with my mother about her life and the things she loved.

The result of putting the selection together has given voice to Elspeth again, and perhaps it serves to illuminate her spirit, too, and the singular vision she had of the world she lived in. There are thoughts on raising children, being married, being widowed, cooking supper, hens, snowdrops, rivers and floods, sunsets, death and day-dreams, unreliable cars, and the incredible passion that words can muster. It's all there, spooled through the faultless sentences she wrote and also spoke in, the humour of which catches a reader unaware and warms the heart long after the pages are closed, the book put away. My mother loved her life, and, as her family, in this first year of grief, knowing that is comforting; her telling us how she saw it, is a gift. No one can really know what their life means to other people, and my mother was unassuming, although her own love of literature showed her the value of reading past writers. Her ability to look both backwards and forwards, and to form thoughts about how and why the ordinary matters, brings us a rich legacy. As was said in one of her obituaries in April 2022, "she was never, ever dull."

In one essay within this collection, Elspeth referred to the "steering [of] one's vehicle along life's motorway." Elspeth's own journey along life's motorway began in Scotland in an echoing Scottish castle where she tamed a jackdaw and often saw the ghost of her grandmother waving from a turret. Her Highland childhood, and her time at boarding school in St. Andrews, are transformed into myth in her only novel, *O Caledonia*, where the misunderstood heroine is murdered on the first page. Even this dramatic fictional event has roots in Elspeth's own real-life preferences. I remember my mother saying while writing the book, "The thing is, I can't stand the name Janet, so the only possibility for this person, now I've got her, is to murder her."

From school, Elspeth's next motorway stop was Oxford, where she assumed an attitude of bohemian glamour and did very little work. She was seventeen and, having read a lot of poetry and espoused various causes, she quickly adopted a style: pale skin, black eyeliner, wild black hair and dramatic clothing, often purple silk or black. This wardrobe would remain with her throughout her life, whether attending events in a muddy pig field in Norfolk or an infamous pub in Soho. Leaving university, Elspeth moved to London and worked part-time in Foyles bookshop and as a waitress in a Lyons Corner House coffee shop. She was remembered by a university friend as "extraordinarily attractive to men," and her own stories of this time included numerous fiancés, as well as a man who said he had married her by proxy and would be taking her back to his home in Nigeria. She avoided this plan by cleverly climbing out of the window at the back of her flat, while her besotted admirer waited at the front door. Instead, she fell in love with George Barker, famous poet and womaniser, whom she had met through his former partner Elizabeth Smart. Elizabeth, whose novel *By Grand Central Station I Sat Down and Wept* was written about her relationship with George, was to become a friend of Elspeth's. But back in the beginning, Elizabeth warned my mother against him. She didn't heed the warning, though; she was taking one of life's leaps of faith and, throwing caution and her upbringing to the wind, she followed her heart with George.

George and Elspeth moved to Norfolk in the late 1960s, and the ramshackle farmhouse they lived in turned out to be her longest stop on life's motorway. Much of that time glimmers in the essays we find in this collection. Life in Norfolk was full and demanding, there was no money, a lot of animals, and five children. She and my father had had a tempestuous relationship. Despite the well-documented setback that he had never been divorced from his first wife, Jessica, and had children with two other women before he and my mother met, they were together until the last. My parents finally married in July 1989, when Jessica had died. My mother said of their marriage, "It just got better and better."

She thought she was an Earth Mother for a while, and embraced bread-making, goat-milking, and the *Guardian*'s Women's Page, which she read on Thursday mornings at the kitchen table, creating a citadel wall of cigarette smoke, pots of tea or glasses of wine, and a death stare directed at her children or anyone else who tried to encroach. It was the seventies; we children lived enthralling lives, free to run wild outside with animals and bicycles, muddy on picnics in the water meadows beyond the garden, then gathering close to home on winter nights when you could see your breath in a cloud in our icy bedrooms. There were power cuts and we stumbled around with lanterns made from swedes, the exoticism of a pumpkin eluding this remote corner of north Norfolk. All of this and so much more is documented in our photograph albums, along with the ghost picture, but it's better evoked by Elspeth's writing.

Years later, when she had become a widow and also a successful writer, Elspeth would sit on a red wooden chair at the kitchen table, a cat moored like a purring barge on the next chair, dogs snoring under the bookshelves behind her while she wrote, sifting through her thoughts and recollections, revisiting the memories and the myths she loved, and reimagining life to show its truths and its pitfalls. *O Caledonia* was published in 1991, after a fiction editor saw an article Elspeth wrote about her hens in a magazine, called "Hens I Have Known," and asked her if she had ever considered writing a novel. She refers to this moment in the essays in this collection, and her belief in the miraculous nature of this happening to her is itself enchanting. Her modesty was a lifelong feature. She was thrilled and astonished by her success; remaining as truly in awe of the magic of the word on the page as she had first been when she fell in love with the idea of the subjunctive as a child, and then with the writing of my father, her poet, before she had ever met him.

The acclaim with which her writing was greeted by publishers, readers, and critics meant that, aged fifty-one and newly widowed, her life changed. She went on a book tour around the world and back, and she had money for the only time in her life. She spent it on horses and an ancient Jaguar. Her unique sense of humour and her lack of ego gained her many friends and fans. As her children, watching her progress in her own right, we enjoyed her success, and joined her in the continuation of the legendary Soho drinking path my father had trodden before. Elspeth, the countrywoman, the shy Scottish linguist, greatly enjoyed the after-parties with other writers at festivals, and post-book-launch drinking sessions, but always only as a contrast to her home life, in Norfolk, in nature with family and animals. She had a knack for the heart of the matter.

On bringing up children, for example, she says, "You need persistence and guile, ruthlessness, resilience, and imagination . . . you must be able to laugh, and above all you must be able to love. All this they teach you. All this you owe to them, and in the end they owe you nothing. They are a privilege beyond accounting."

Because she wrote what she lived and lived what she wrote, she is alive in her writing, whether journalism or fiction. Revisiting these essays and stories now after the success of *O Caledonia* is in itself a metaphysical experience. Elspeth was a classicist, mother, wife, pig fancier, dog lover, countrywoman, terrible driver, and bona fide spellmaker. These pieces show her in her daily life and, more than that, they show her in the relationship her life had with her imagination. None of her writing was ordinary, and neither was she; she had a facility for scattering *jeux d'esprit* across the surface of everyday experience, and she lived a love affair with words that has not ended with her death.

In my family, stories are treasures; incident and experience unwrapped and examined, retold and held up against the light so every grain of thought and word is shared. They are like Christmas baubles, burnished by frequent handling, the gleam of revisited memory reflecting all our yesterdays back to us, again and again; as bright and vivid as if we have just lived them, yet also linking the moment of retelling back so far into the past that there is no knowing where anything began, or if it will ever end.

This liminal place is where Elspeth has existed since her death in April 2022. Reading her now is a privilege for me: I can see how much she loved her life, her family, her world. And I am glad to know this. Now she is no longer physically present, these essays and stories allow her to be among us. She would like that, she even set it up, really, saying of her own grief when my father died, "I find death absolutely unacceptable and I cannot come to terms with it. I can no more conceive of utter extinction, of never, than I can of infinity. I cannot believe that all that passion, wit, eloquence, and rage can be deleted by something so vulgar as the heart stopping."

Her words jump from the page and straight inside me, they linger in the air as if she has simply paused, mid-thought, and left the room for a moment to answer the telephone or find another bottle of the Bulgarian vintage. She doesn't come back into the room, and yet she is here. I know her, I feel her heart, an earthly and eternal warmth, her mind, with diamond-graven clarity, and I also feel her spirit around me, ethereal, complex, and eternal. I have learned from her how to re-examine treasured stories, drawn by the lustre that gleams from these pages. I understand how she swoops between past and present to weave a future in her words. There is always that something in her writing that makes me feel she is talking, just to me, right now. Just as she looks at me, the light in her eyes undimmed, gazing out of the photograph of our family and our animals in the cart shed in the rain. Today she says this, about Claws, her childhood jackdaw:

The most marvellous of all his gifts to me was in essence metaphysical. I would see him, a dark speck among the tumbling clouds, and call his name, three times always, and see him swoop from the heavens in an unfaltering ellipse to my shoulder. To call a bird from the air is so extraordinary, rivalled in my experience only by the appearance of one's abstractions of thoughts and images in the tangible form of a book. And even then, the bird wins.

Yes. The bird wins. But the pages are pretty good too.

Raffaella Barker
Cley, Norfolk, September 2022

PART 1

CHILDHOOD

AND

SCOTLAND

BIRDS OF EARTH AND AIR

With what a commotion of wings and legs and beaks and damp earth do we come thudding into the world. Thank you, friendly stork. As for leaving, we hope to be ushered hence by flights of angels. In the interim the plumed ones weave their mysterious ways through our lives. The Roman armies carried sacred chickens into the battlefield and much was made of the scatter of corn from their beaks as they stamped their excitement at feeding time (*tripudium solistimum*)—literally, the most perfect stamping. The flights and cries and formations of birds informed the augurs of divine censure or approval; birds encountered on journeys were significant too, as indeed they are now. Do we not feel chosen, blessed even, by a heron rowing its way across the heavens, an owl's motionless glare from a pine branch, the harping outstretched flight of swans? Are we not accursed by the single magpie? How hard it is to break the curse by crossing oneself and spitting, while steering one's vehicle along life's motorway.

The crowing of the cock at Gethsemane or indeed in any early morning may betoken disaster one way or another; they crow by day and they crow by night and they just don't care, although some people do, especially those who have left the city for the great enfolding peace of the countryside. Pigeons make a lot of noise too in the country. Londoners are rude and uncaring about these fine birds.

Although we do eat them out here in the rural, their great confusion of cooing is one of summer's most divine orchestrations. On an August night in Northumberland I watched shooting stars plunge across the black sky and woke at dawn to massed choirs of pigeons in fugue: "I mourn, I mourn," calling and calling over and again "for my love, my love, my love." By day I climbed the hill and found myself on Flodden Field where one summer afternoon in 1513 the English hacked to pieces the Scottish king and his nobles, the Flowers of the Forest. It was all over by teatime. Still the birds sob in the woods.

For myself, my first objective memory, outside the dim, cosy nursery world, is of a bird, a huge white seagull perched, motionless and marmoreal, on top of the drawing room door. We children had been plucked from our beds and brought down to see him; he stared sideways at us from an unwinking angry golden eye.

———

My father came from a long line of parrot-keeping men. From his infancy, around 1913, he could remember a white cockatoo who had campaigned with Wellington's "infamous army" in 1815. This bird, almost a century old, spoke, or rather swore, in a version of English long gone from the world, just distinguishable, and as my father put it, fruity. His own parrot, an African grey called Punlel, did not swear but enjoyed a spot of sarcasm—"very funny, very funny, that's very funny, goodnight." He bit female children. My grandfather's African grey also bit female children, and when he first bit me, aged four, I was violently sick into his cage. Punlel, some twenty-five years later, bit my four-year-old daughter, who reacted identically. A delightful moment of mother-and-daughter communion. Pun slalomed expertly about the dining table and with his harsh African cries terrorised the gentle Scottish garden birds as he patrolled the lawns. You will have heard of them, mavis, laverock, and throstle. When he was nineteen years old, Pun laid an egg. It was too late then for us to re-create him in Eve's image, and he continued his transgender life for a further three decades.

———

Where I grew up there were jackdaws everywhere, in the trees, in the chimneys, and all too often in the fire. "Suttee?" quavered my grandmother, who had lived long in India. The bird I have loved most was a jackdaw. I found him in long wet grass, crying most piteously, a tiny pink form almost entirely composed of a gaping cross-billed mouth. Perhaps he had been flung from his tree-top nest because of the crossed bill, or perhaps the fall had caused it. Anyhow, in the way of children of those days, I brought him in and kept him warm in a haybox, and fed him from the back of a silver mustard spoon. Astonishingly, he survived, became fledged, learned to fly and catch beetles in his crossed bill. I took him back then to become a bird in the pine grove where I found him and he soared up into the dark branches. I sat alone in my bedroom; with a heavy heart I contemplated his empty box and the traces of down caught in the hay; before the first tear had rolled the length of my cheek, he was at the window, tapping. He was always completely free to come and go as he pleased, and he remained with me for eleven years, taking off from my lofty sill into the windy skies or mounting enjoyable raids on the jackdaw colonials in the countless chimney pots; he would march round the edge of the chimney poking his head in and screeching until the inmates lost patience and emerged in a great furious fluster to pursue him back to the triumphant safety of my open window. My room became a guano-ridden cavern and my books to this day bear his mark; some have torn pages, too, for he had no time for reading and would rip the paper impatiently. Henry James and Jane Austen drew particular hostility. Everywhere possible he went with me, perched on my shoulder, or flying ahead and back and round in circles. My horse became resentfully accustomed to his presence on her withers. In the car he was happy to travel on my lap, but there were journeys on which he was unwelcome, like the eighty-mile round trip to the dentist. Then, and only then, he was a dreadful nuisance, pursuing the car and trying to settle on the bonnet like a parody of the Rolls-Royce nymph. In the end I removed my little sisters' doll's house and made it into a holding centre for these occasions.

The castle staircase was immense, rising in stately measure from the vaulted entrance hall and gradually narrowing as it spiralled upwards, all grim grey stone. Claws, as I called him, never flew up or downstairs, but hopped his way, step by step, a sight immeasurably poignant, reminding me of Catullus's heartbreaking image of his mistress's dead pet bird on its dark path to the underworld, hopping too. The most marvellous of all his gifts to me was in essence metaphysical. I would see him, a dark speck among the tumbling clouds, and call his name, three times always, and see him swoop from the heavens in an unfaltering ellipse to my shoulder. To call a bird from the air is so extraordinary, rivalled in my experience only by the appearance of one's abstraction of thoughts and images in the tangible form of a book. And even then, the bird wins.

From the beginning, Punlel and Claws chose to ignore each other; one afternoon they ignored each other a little too much and collided on the luncheon table. Pun was executing a daring skiing manoeuvre and Claws as usual was tripping from plate to plate, helping himself with undiscriminating relish from grey mounds of well-cooked cabbage and tremulous orange jelly. A cross-billed jackdaw enjoying orange jelly is a painterly sight; words like *shard*, *stipple*, *lucent*, even *chiaroscuro* leap to the lip. (A Labrador engaged on a Hobnob is good, too.) The impact was shocking to both birds and resulted in synchronised shrieking, feather loss, broken china, and a temporary ban from family meals.

At the sea, my parents had a normal house, which they reached each summer after a migration of insane proportions, involving cars, trains, a carrier lorry, baggage rolls containing blankets and saucepans and supplementary furniture and cooking devices and cages, on the just-in-case principle which makes life so difficult.

All the animals, birds, fish, and reptiles came, as well as we five children, Nanny, Nanny's helper, and Nanny's sister. I have horrible memories of the horses escaping from the train and galloping down the railway line, and the scrabble of the tortoises' claws against the floor of their box as the train swung over the perilous Tay Bridge. My jackdaw enjoyed these holidays, cruising low along the beach over picnicking families; how envious they were when he landed on our rug. He slept always on the end of my bed and his still brooding form in the twilight gave me a great desire to teach him to say "Never more." Imagine my astonishment when he interrupted my patient repetitions of this phrase and said "Never mind" in a patronising, manly voice. This was the evil doing of my brother. "Never mind" was all Claws ever said and, as my brother pointed out, it is a more useful phrase than "Never more."

One spring he started bringing things, leaves and twigs and feathers and scissors, and setting them in my pocket. Then he climbed into my pocket and stared at me sideways and twisted his head about as if beckoning. A quick referral to Lorenz's *King Solomon's Ring* told me that Claws was offering me matrimony. My first ever proposal; my truest lover. *O lacrimae rerum.*

He might have lived for fifty years or more had I not at last betrayed him by leaving home to seek my fortune. My sisters offered love and care but he would have none. For a few weeks he hardly stirred from my empty chamber. Then one bitter winter morning he flew repeatedly into the castle wall and killed himself.

Other birds have shaped my life in other ways. As an indolent and bookish child, I used to hide in the henhouse and read all afternoon while my parents thought I was out in the fresh air building dams. The hens were friendly enough but they died away swiftly in the jaws of the golden retriever and his vigorous assistant, the Irish terrier. Then the dogs were obliged to wear the hens' corpses slung around their necks to teach them a lesson. They did not learn their lesson, and soon I had the henhouse to myself. I made it into a delightful secret study with cardboard box bookshelves, a torch, exercise books, and bottles of Quink. Thus began my literary life.

Years later, and many birds later, a piece I wrote, about hens I have known, for a Sunday newspaper, inspired a publisher to suggest a novel. I could say a great deal about interesting hens, and also about owls; my mother, from time to time, raised baby owls in her tower, untroubled by their disgusting eating habits. But dwelling as one does in time and space, one must call it a day. I shall mention only that in Crete the tiny owl *Strix* marks the passing of darkness into dawn with a final melodious single yelp; immediately after this comes the first crow of the cock, the first bray of the ass. Here in Norfolk three delightful Indian Runner ducks have joined me. They live in the garden where my American spouse makes busy, fetching bowls of snails for their degustation; they require that he crack the shells.

I am hoping to persuade them to move occasionally in graceful single file up and down the stairs; they will show to great advantage against the yellow wall. And when winter begins we plan a pair of Muscovies to warm our laps for Sunday evening television.

FIFE

The Ancient Kingdom of Fife forms a blunt peninsula which shoulders out into the North Sea, bounded on one side by the Firth of Forth. Driving up from Edinburgh, you used to take the ferry across, under the shadow of the mighty railway bridge, where men suspended in little baskets were eternally repainting, eternally and fruitlessly, for as soon as they reached the end they had to start again.

Battleships and submarines gleamed in the shifting sunlight and sometimes a school of porpoises performed acrobatics beyond the ferry's wake. Cars were assisted on and off board by a turntable which pointed them in the right direction, leaving no chance of driver error. This was a relief to me, for the whelming deep washed voraciously onto the end of the pier and was all too visible through the many fissures of the ramps. Sweet and green, the hills of Fife welcomed us like a benison.

So it was in those days. Now traffic goes roaring over the Forth Road Bridge, which takes time off the journey but mars the significance of crossing the water, the sense of entering another land. The coastal villages and small towns, however, have not changed very much. Kirkcaldy, home of linoleum, still smells deliciously of linseed oil; Leven sprawls more than it did, and has an air of loucheness uncharacteristic of cleanly East Fife. Nearby are the caves of Wemyss and their Bronze Age drawings; here you may see the earliest depictions of a boat to be found in these islands. There used to be boatyards all along this stretch, with seagulls marching proprietorially over the great vaulting wooden ribs which dominated the quaysides.

In Largo, Alexander Selkirk was born; it was he who so enraged his fellow mariners that they dumped him on the island of Juan Fernandez. After four years of solitude he was rescued, and recycled for posterity as Robinson Crusoe. But for me this is all peripheral.

Two places form the heartland of my Fife, and the first of these is Elie. Elie is an old fishing village; its houses, many of them crowstepped and gabled, border a wide, curving bay. At one end of the bay looms the harbour and gaunt stone granary; at the other end Elie has merged into Earlsferry. A dark and rock-strewn headland encloses the pale shore. Round the point lies another bay, then more cliffs, higher and menacing. Here Macduff took to a boat and fled from Macbeth across the water, leaving his family behind:

> The Thane of Fife had a wife
> Where is she now?

Macduff evidently knew where he was going. As a child I assumed that the smudge of land you could sometimes see on the far horizon was Abroad. Abroad was only visible when rain was threatening and the light inky and lurid.

I had a great fear of war, and when the occasional plane came droning over from that inscrutable foreign land (in fact, the coastline of North Berwick) I would flatten myself in the dunes, and hold my breath and pray until the danger had passed.

Almost everything that I remember of Elie centres around the beach. It is a perfect place for little children. They play now as I did, as my father did a hundred years ago. Sandcastles, digging to Australia, rock pools and shrimping nets. Nothing has changed; there is no promenade, no commercial aid to maritime pleasure. The faded beach huts are still dotted along the shore. One of the excitements of New Year was always the abrupt departure of these huts into the massive January tides which came lashing over the sea wall, drowning the harbour road and seriously inconveniencing the clientele of the Ship Inn. Once a derelict whale rolled up on the sands. We were not allowed to go near it on the grounds that it might explode. Eventually it was removed on a system of rollers and ropes, dragged by eight Clydesdale cart horses.

On the far side of the harbour is another bay, known as Ruby Bay, where a ship of the Spanish Armada, blown far off course, spilled a cargo of rubies onto the sea bed. To this day, children still find their glowing fragments scattered about the shore among the white cowrie shells and black bladder wrack. A slope of grass, starry with thrift, climbs towards the lighthouse and the Lady's Tower, once a discreet bathing place.

In summer, Mr. Haig's beach ponies used to plod tirelessly up and down the central bay. They wore scarlet or yellow harness and jingling bells; their saddles had horns to hold on to. Sometimes a fluffy foal frisked alongside and one year there was a black baby donkey. To belong to the select band whom Mr. Haig allowed to lead the ponies on their threepenny or sixpenny treks was every child's ambition. It was my first taste of elitism. The other great attraction in the summer months was the Children's Special Service Mission, known as the Cism. Each morning we laboured with buckets and spades and built a great altar and studded it with arabesques of shells and frondy whorls of seaweed. Then we sat behind it on the warm, soft sand and sang:

"I'm H.A.P.P.Y., I'm H.A.P.P.Y.,
I know I am, I'm sure I am,
I'm H.A.P.P.Y."

Beyond the altar the gulls swooped and cried, the sea glittered, and the day dazzled with promise. Life was a sunlit dream where you wore your bathing suit all the time.

As children grow older, they require danger. The cliffs at the end of West Bay are wild, slippery, and lethal. To clamber round them you need nerve and expertise, neither of which I had. Nonetheless I forced myself along tiny ledges above jagged, gurgling gullies, clung to the towering basalt pillars, leapt inelegantly over chasms. It was always terrifying, and it was always thrilling.

Seals play in the waters here, and flocks of cormorants skim through the waves or stand motionless on the rocks. The water is very deep, translucent, and green as glass. Behind Elie, there is an old and hallowed golf course, but it never attracted me. My brother, my enemy, used to whirl his driver round his head, let go, and send it hurtling like a cruise missile straight at me. Golf balls whistled past my temples. No thanks.

Gradually, too, the beach lost its charms for me. I became a fat sullen teenager who refused to be seen in a bathing suit. I sat scowling on the sand while my little sisters dug and delved with infant absorption. The bright sea wind baked the scowl onto my face; once it stayed there for thirty-six hours. Although I continued to join in my family's mammoth, thrice-yearly migration from our home in the north to the house by the sea, it was against my will and I remember nothing of those times apart from the insane scale of the operation, which involved five children, nannies, dogs, the chief cat, budgerigars, tortoises, goldfish, a parrot, a jackdaw, and for a while two horses, who travelled by train until the day when they escaped and wrought havoc at Elie Station. Thereafter they were banned from seaside holidays. Lucky them, I thought. Only when I had children of my own did I realise again what an enchantment I had wilfully lost.

Elie has a southerly aspect. A chain of small fishing villages leads northward, round the point of Fife Ness towards St. Andrews. Each of these villages, St. Monans, Pittenweem, Anstruther, has its own grave charm like Elie; though they have their share of winter's blast, in my recollection they are always sunlit, bright with the impulse of the moment, the gull swooping, a blue boat lifting on the wave, the slap of water on the jetty. They are also pragmatic. Near the tip of the peninsula, Crail has many of the summer delights of those other villages, but is hard going in winter. Robert Louis Stevenson, who took some pleasure in Scotland's desolate places, found Crail too much for him: "This grey, grim, sea beaten hole," he wrote.

Once you round the tip you are onto the northern outlook and St. Andrews is another matter altogether. Its shattered towers, gaunt and spectral on their rocky headland, stare unforgivingly northwards to the Arctic. On still days the haar, the mist off the North Sea, drifts inland, enfolding and darkening the tall stone houses, casting a dank gleam on the slate roofs; beads of moisture cling to your hair, and you ponder the phrase "chilled to the bone."

Or sky and sea merge and the tossing gulls are indistinguishable from the foam flinging up off the waves. Then the east wind comes whipping in sheer and sharp, freighted with the snows of Siberia. At night in bed you can't sleep for thinking of those lines from Wordsworth's "The Idiot Boy":

> His teeth, they chatter, chatter still,
> Like a loose casement in the wind.

You will never be warm again. Conversely, if you decide you can bear it no longer, and go to the beguiling, decadent South (England), you will not need an overcoat for many years—not until that primal immunity has worn off. All this I know because I spent four years at boarding school in St. Andrews. Enough of that. There is a great deal more to St. Andrews than the plaint of a shivering schoolgirl.

Mary, Queen of Scots came here, staying in a room which is part of my old school's library. As her ship neared the lowering, wind-beaten cliffs, according to William Shakespeare:

the rude sea grew civil at her song
And certain stars shot madly from their spheres
To hear the sea maid's music.

Some would have it that these lines refer to certain political displacements. I prefer the image as it is. What music? "Plaisir d'Amour" would suit. The doomed queen planted a hawthorn tree in the grounds of the ancient university, the oldest in Britain after Oxford and Cambridge. The hawthorn lives on, couchant rather than rampant, lovingly supported. The university has brought forth many great scholars, not least of them Andrew Lang:

St. Andrews by the Northern Sea
A haunted town it is to me,

he wrote, and he found Oxford something of a disappointment later. The students' scarlet gowns mingle and separate around the grey buildings in a poignant counterpoint. Youth and age, colour and its absence. My grandfather studied divinity here, here my parents met when they were students. The scarlet gown hung on the back of our nursery door, but not one of us took it up.

St. Andrews is to me a city (and it is a cathedral city, not a town) plangent with regrets and sorrows. The past has seen terrible violence, murders, beheadings, and burnings at the stake. You can still see the window in the ruins of the castle from which Cardinal Beaton, lolling on silken cushions, surveyed the Protestant martyrs as they turned to charred bones.

The emphasis on the silken cushions is peculiarly St. Andrean. Would the scene have been any less horrible if he had knelt on the cold stone window ledge? The presence of the church dominates St. Andrews, even in these secular days. Like Oxford, it is a city of tolling bells.

Its very bleakness is fraught with wild romance; it is the perfect setting for a tragic love affair, Héloïse and Abelard or Tristan and Iseult. If you walk towards the city along the West Sands, you will see it in its most sorrowful beauty. This is one of the great views of the world. It is both a *memento mori* and a monument to endurance.

I suppose I must also mention that St. Andrews is the golfer's Mecca. And summer comes there, and the sun does shine.

But these are not my concerns. One of these days I hope to become a ghost. Then I will float above the shadowy seals and dancing waves of Elie, and I will drift with the haar about the towers of St. Andrews.

THE DRIVER'S SEAT

My first driving lesson took place twenty-four years before I passed my driving test. My capacity for cowardice, irresolution, and day-dreaming thus enabled me to experience, though not enjoy, lessons and tests throughout the late fifties, the sixties, the seventies, and on into the early eighties. As I lurched and stalled from decade to decade two constancies went with me: the certain failure of the test and the heartrending optimism of my ever-changing instructors. This time, they promised, things would be different; this time I would be calm, alert, and competent. Alertness, however, is not given to us all, and optimism soon faded to stoic resignation, clenched knuckles, despondency, and madness. It was just like learning maths all over again.

However, on the bright December morn of that first lesson, I knew nothing of this. Soon, I imagined, I might be motoring southwards, down the pale dusty roads of Provence, some demon lover stashed silently and admiringly beside me.

So it was that with modest hope I clambered into the small grey Austin parked outside our house. It was difficult to get in because I was wearing my only pair of high heels in case my legs looked fat, and I was conscious of my siblings' jeering faces plastered against an upstairs window. Mr. Methven's bald pate dazzled in the frosty sunlight. He looked at my shoes. "Ye'll need to take those off," he said. I kicked them insouciantly in front of me. One lodged under the accelerator pedal.

Sighing, he leaned over and chucked them into the back. He told me about the gears. My mind was racing. What was wrong with my shoes? Could I drive in slippery nylons? Why were there three pedals when you only had two feet? Slippery nylon feet. Would the pedals ladder my nylons? "Look in the mirror," he commanded. What now? I looked and saw only a stretch of icy empty road. I twisted it sideways and peered at my pallid freckled face. It didn't look much worse than usual. What was the matter with him? He yanked the mirror back into position. "Thon is for the *road*, for *oncoming traffic*. Ye're no in the boudoir now, Madame."

I realised I hadn't been listening to what he said about the gears. He went through it all again. Eventually, after a number of false starts, we moved off, veering erratically about the village street. "Look in the mirror," he yelled again. I looked. There was a car behind us. Shaking with fear, I slammed on the brake. We both shot forwards. The car behind drove past, its driver making the V for Victory sign. All was well. I ventured to look at Mr. Methven. His face was contorted and his scalp was no longer dazzling, more a rosy pink; its texture too seemed changed, velours, perhaps, I thought. "What the hell did ye do that for?" "Well, just to let him past. That's all right, isn't it? He seemed pleased." "No, it is not. No, he was not."

On we went through the village. The legions of the damned were out, determined that I should run them over. People, bicycles, dogs, parked cars, moving cars. Had they no sense? Why weren't they indoors? How I hated them. The motorist requires an empty road. At last we reached the open country. What a relief. But now there were bends. Bends are dangerous. You can't see round them. Mr. Methven was getting angry again. "Will ye kindly go into top gear. And stay there." Top gear was far too fast, anyone could see that. And how could I possibly concentrate on driving when he wouldn't stop talking, on and on about eye, hand, foot co-ordination. Wasn't there a disease like that, something caught off rats in the trenches? Had Mr. Methven been in the trenches? Round another bend we sped in demoniac fourth gear. Ahead was a vertical drop, a glacier snaking to St. Andrews Bay and certain death. I braked violently, the car skidded sideways, stalled, and fell silent with its nose embedded in the bank. A storm of lapwings rose from the kale field, crowding the sky with omen. In silence Mr. Methven got out and fetched his spade from the boot. In silence we heaved and shoved and shoved and heaved. At last we had the car facing homewards. My shoeless feet were frozen and lacerated, coated in mud and grit. As I drove back I felt a warm trickle of blood ooze from my big toe, down the clutch pedal, onto the dove-grey carpet. The pain was almost pleasant.

In the village street, the thought of Mr. Methven and my parents and my future in driving caused me to shake again. "Change down, change down," he yelled. The schoolchildren were waiting for their bus. We passed them in a series of convulsive lurches, jerking back and forth like a pair of marionettes, heads grotesquely nodding. "Go into neutral. Put the brake on." I grabbed the gear stick, yanked. Out it came into my desperate fist, meek as a flower. I pulled on the handbrake, switched off the engine, and handed the gear stick to its owner.

"I think I'll no be seeing you again next Tuesday," he said. In the event we never met again, for a couple of weeks later, returning from Hogmanay revelries, Mr. Methven was killed on that self-same glacier above the sea.

PACKING FOR INDIA

It wasn't snowing, but it might have been. So great a stillness surrounded the house, the air chilled with presentiment, the blank sky tinged mauve, the hills guarding their own. I had come from a long way into that cold afternoon; already my life in another country was cut off, and the people who crowded it had moved into memory; they were people I used to know. This house held the present, the unforgiving minute, the fleeting untenable last of a life; our mother's deathbed. We wanted time to stop so that her life might not end. We wanted it all to be over, too. Arm in arm, fear and boredom stalked the bedroom, and guilt followed at their heels. A terrier perhaps, with sharp little snappity jaws. The real dogs, two huge mastiffs, leaned against the bed, one on each side; damp muzzles probed the counterpane, eyes rolled in anxious devotion. The Marie Curie nurses hated to see these enormous beasts, constantly in their way, and banished them to the garden, closing the curtains against their reproachful stares. Our mother ignored the presence of the nurses; if obliged to acknowledge them she would treat them as slightly unwelcome friends of my sisters. For she was not ill at all, just resting after a nasty cold, and enjoying a little holiday away from her cats. Her morphine was dropped into tiny glasses of peach juice, secretly, for she certainly would have refused to take it. She drifted in and out of consciousness, sometimes feigning sleep, sometimes alert, sometimes both.

I saw her stroke a nurse's cashmere sleeve (the nurses all wore plain clothes and in the Scottish borders that means cashmere and tweed). "Nice fluffy dog," said Mother. The nurse gazed bleakly at the wall; two thick lucent strands of slobber, witness to the expelled mastiffs, were inching slowly down the paintwork. "Filthy great brutes," she muttered, not quite under her breath. "Will you be off soon?" Mother enquired, her eyes iceberg blue. "I'll be right away as soon as I've got my coat and boots." "Where do you live?" "Hawick." "What a bore for you." Grim in her coat and boots, Nurse hurried through the hall and kitchen and disappeared into the capacious darkness of the walk-in drinks cupboard, briskly closing the door on our cries of goodnight and thank you and not that way. Silently she emerged and was gone out into the squalling sleet. She shouted something like "See you tomorrow," but in the event she did not return.

We took turns, the sisters and I, to sit with our mother so that she was never alone by night or day. Her window looked out to the high bare hills and the shifting clouds. In the morning the mist would lift in swathes and leave drops of water on the sword-shaped *Crocosmia* leaves beneath the sill. The hens scratched about the flowerbed and sipped the shining beads. She couldn't see them from her pillows, but when I told her, her face lit. "Yes, that's what they do." There were no mirrors in the room. I wondered whether this was deliberate, for her face was slightly distorted by cancer, only very slightly. She could not have moved from her bed to look in the mirror. Perhaps a mirror would have prompted recollection and sorrow. No one will know.

She was one of those women who even in old age retain a certain girlishness. The illness had reduced her, made her doll-like, but she was a faded and ravaged girl-doll, not an old-woman-doll, and evanescent glamour clung about her. On the end of the bed were propped, with difficulty, postcards, cuttings, and photographs as demanded. Miss Anastasia Noble and two of her deerhounds, a seaside village where once we lived—"Let's go there tomorrow!"—a holy cow in India. There were no pictures of any of us; just as well, I reflected, as I would not have appeared in them. Never once in childhood did any photograph of me stand among the others on her bedroom mantelpiece. But this was no time for ancient grievances. I thought that every minute, however fraught or tedious or just plain awkward, should be cherished for her. The intense pleasure she drew from the hens and their raindrops, the colour and texture of a grape, the cloud shadows on the hills, a cat's mask watchful at the curtain's edge, should be remarked, captured, and contained. Perhaps most of all she enjoyed the gathering in her room in early morning. We would be elated that she had got through the night. Inconsequential talk, giggling, tea and toast for us, morphine and peach juice for her, while something of the dormitory obtained and something of what she called "shoe-kicking time"—an hour for the exchange of secrets and intimacies, which, unlike my sisters, I had avoided always. What confidences could I ever have shared? I, a spinster and a treacherous exile. I thought about the rows and distances there had been between us, and how they didn't at all matter now, at least to me. This was how we knew each other, and it was all right. My sisters had happier times with her, and that was all right too.

In these early mornings, when she is strongest, she is talking about her own childhood, in Scotland, but mostly in India. Why did she never tell us all this before? She is a small child, sitting on the warm red earth, watching the potter and his wheel. The red mud is shining and a white cow walks slowly down the hill path towards them. The potter slaps the clay. Her ayah smiles. A slow bird passes beside them through the sky; they are so high on the hill that birds are flying beneath them too. The cow calls out and now it is the sound of the great ship, moving down the Clyde into evening and starlight with a thousand little boats all round it. The people she doesn't know are waving and she is waving back. So much waving, so many faces glimpsed and gone into night or sea mist, so many journeys. A dark face now, coming from the shadows of the big white house, on to the verandah. The dark person brings a tray across the lawn. The child is sitting far away with her mother at a wobbly table under a spreading tree. Men are draped about the tree's wide branches; they swing their legs and laugh.

Her ayah is there too; she never laughs but she is always smiling. Oh, then something bad happened. She will tell us about that another morning. Now she will sleep.

————

In sleep she cried out sometimes for our father; he had died two years before. Sometimes she was so deeply still that I thought she had gone and I was almost downcast when she stirred, and then I was shocked at myself and ashamed to find the long time of her passing unbearable. She grew smaller through those long October afternoons. In such profound sleep, her head tilted sideways and down towards her chest, she seemed perfectly closed and withdrawn, setting forth herself down a wide river towards the sea, over the rolling waters, not drowning but going very privately adrift. For a moment, just before it dipped behind the hills, the sun would send ripples of riverine light up and down the bedroom walls and over her quiet face. Then it was gone and the sky had blanched; jackdaws flocked across it, jostling their way to their roost in the tower. Until darkness fell the air was raucous with their squabbles. You become used to this quiet life, sequestered in the hills, the wind and the wail of the kettle, the dogs outside barking when the doctor comes, and the downstairs rooms all shadow and closed curtains so the dogs cannot see the doctor. Our mother thinks or claims to think that the doctor's visits are entirely social. Perhaps they are, for he is supposedly on holiday, like her, and he walks with his Labrador up the two-mile track to the house. The mastiffs don't mind the Labrador, only the doctor. It is another world where small incidents stand in sharp relief against a muted, dreamy background. You don't want to look too much into this background; you know what is there; it could come out at any moment.

She tells us, one morning, about her ayah, who was being brought with them all back to Scotland. She died on the boat. She was wrapped in a Union Jack and the ship's officers dropped her slowly, on a long chain, into the sea. Everyone stood in church clothes on the deck and they sang "Abide with Me." But the ayah didn't abide; away she went, whirling and brightly coloured, into the grey waves. I imagine dim shrouded forms enfolded gently in the brown shining Ganges. Rivers of death, rivers of forgetting, the clay dissolving. The sea seems very cold, too cold for the ayah.

———

This afternoon Mother says quite suddenly, straight out of sleep, "There's a hare on the ceiling." And there is. The shadows cast upwards by a huge vase of flowers, brilliant gold and scarlet gerbera, are compounded into a perfect semblance of a hare, angular, dark and graceful, stilled in mid-leap. I am half asleep myself, and I am alarmed now to see her sitting up with astonishing ease. "I used to be able to pack for India in twenty minutes!" she says. "I must find my things. I need my white slacks. And my red shoes. I think they're over there." She points to a corner full of dust. She starts to move her legs towards the side of the bed. She intends to get up. She must not do this. She cannot do this. She is a stick-woman. She is an old girl-doll. She will break in pieces. Oh no, she is a girl who is packing for India.

"Stay there, sit still, I'll find everything," I say. "No you won't. Just don't. You'll be in the way. You don't know what I want. And you never were the helpful sort." Her voice has been strong but it is ebbing now. She whispers. "I must have my red shoes. I want to wear them." I hear the kettle begin its moaning in the kitchen. Someone is there. I rush out, find a sister, and rush back. Our mother is muttering about missing the boat. Together, after a protracted slow-motion struggle, we restrain her, flatten her, tuck her in tight, and try to make her listen to Radio 4. This doesn't work well. "Too English." She is still anxious that she will miss the boat. She still wants her red shoes. A flurry of snow patters against the window, the evening nurse arrives, the jackdaws float by. Another day gone forever.

———————

So there we are one late autumn afternoon, my sisters, their daughters, and me. We are decorating the church for the funeral, bronze bracken and rosehips, berries red and black, leafy branches from the hollows where the deer sleep. A huge wind is rising and beating about the valley, about the ancient kirk. As the light wanes, the waters of the burn rise; we can hear them roaring now, but we think little of it. Next day dawns, cheerless and wild. The birds are blown horizontally across the white sky. The steep terraced garden is filled with floodwater; tree tops poke up into the drenching rain. The great rivers have burst their banks and every valley is flooded. The funeral cannot take place. All the roads from England are closed. Like further straggles of storm-tossed birds, the black-clad mourners hover uncertainly about the house. By nightfall they are planning departure. No one can wait around for a burial of undecided date. Bloody Marys take over the evening. Sleepers sag from chairs, the mastiffs slumber against knees, their heads propped on the dining room table. The wind drops, but not much.

Days pass and the waters recede. We gather in depleted numbers at the church, where the bracken and rowan and hips are still bright. The minister reads Tennyson's last poem, "Crossing the Bar."

> But such a tide as moving seems asleep,
> Too full for sound and foam,
> When that which drew from out the boundless deep
> Turns again home.

Her grandsons carry her coffin to the grave. We stand about it and the minister speaks of sure and certain knowledge. The hills seem to have moved forward. They rise huge above us and the grave is brimful of water. The water reflects the hills. They are suspended there upside down and in the very depths of the grave there is a flash of sunlit sky. The minister swathes the coffin, which is very small, in the blue-and-white flag of Saint Andrew, the Saltire. The oldest great-granddaughter begins to howl; she clutches her mother's skirts. Her five siblings follow suit. They form a broad-based pyramid of lamentation. The wet flowers which lie about the grave's edge like a bridal quilt are shining after the rain. Every holy word has been spoken and she has been consigned to the earth and life everlasting, but she is not in the earth. Nor is she on the water which might have borne her gracefully downwards as it subsided. We have to leave her there unburied. We move off in little groups, all turning back to her. A small ship stranded among flowers, beside the water, beneath the trees, below the hills.

As we go down the track to the narrow road, a woman touches my arm and murmurs words of condolence. It is the nurse who walked into the drinks cupboard. "If I could just call in one day," she is saying, "I don't know if you'll have seen them. I left them that last night and I never got back. I think they were in your mum's bedroom, in the corner. My red shoes."

PART 2

ADULT LIFE:
GEORGE
AND
CHILDREN

DOGS OF ATHENS

It was in Athens airport that I saw them first. They sat close together, very upright on their airport chairs, all knitting. Or were they all knitting? As I walked past it seemed out of the corner of my eye as though only one was knitting and the others were straightening the wool, holding the ball, but each taking her turn with the needles. Three ancient crones, wrapped in black. The Three Fates, Clotho, Lachesis, and something. Why couldn't I remember the third one's name? It is depressing to survive for fifty years only to begin to forget things you have always known. "Well," says the voice in the back of my head, "if only you hadn't drunk so much ouzo at Iraklion before you got on the plane things might be different." "Rubbish," I tell it. "Flying is awful, crazy, degrading to human dignity. Remember Icarus drowning in the sea we've just crossed. There are warnings everywhere and we should take some notice." "Flying is the safest form of transport," says the voice. It says this often. "Qantas has never lost a passenger," it adds. "What's

Qantas got to do with flying Crete to Athens, or Athens to London, come to that?" I demand. I peer anxiously at the Three Fates, for tomorrow is another flying day. They ignore me, intent on their skeins of orange wool. Ravelling and unravelling. May the Lord preserve us. Anyway, I have outwitted them for now.

I become aware that there are a number of cheerful dogs about apparently unattached, trotting around the concourses, greeting pilots and vigorously enjoying the business of international arrivals and departures and casual disposal of airport food. How they smile and swish their tails; east, west, dogs are best and I am missing mine. Tomorrow I will see them. Today and now there is the hotel and then Christina.

I didn't know Christina very well although I'd seen her on and off over many years. Back in England it had seemed a good idea to stop over one night in Athens, meet, have fun. Christina hadn't actually sounded very enthusiastic down the phone, but her laconic and curiously well preserved Texan drawl had often misled me. Now she was in hospital and I'd no idea what was wrong. She had sent a message to the hotel saying, "Come this minute, bored, bored, bored." The hospital was up in the hills outside Athens and I was pleased to have discovered the bus station and the bus despite the intense pall of mid-afternoon heat and the major handicap of my fifth-century BC Attic Greek. One of the people I had accosted for directions had insisted in only slightly American English that no one had used the rough breathing since AD 400. That wasn't going to stop me.

As the suburbs fell away the bus gathered speed into dusty scrubland. The sky hung heavy and dull over slopes littered with unfinished breeze-block structures; in the hazed light they seemed like ruined temples, parched and skeletal. I looked forward to the cool of evening and the hotel roof garden where I might sip a Bloody Mary or two and gaze out at the ghostly Parthenon. I realised that not knowing what was wrong with Christina had no relevance; she probably wouldn't tell me anyway. If she even knew. She had a dismissive attitude to the woes of the body. I remembered her galloping through the woods on a huge grey horse, her skirts bundled up round her thighs, one broken arm in plaster and sling. She admitted to hangovers; nothing much else. And she disposed of hangovers with a slosh of brandy in the morning's second cup of coffee, followed by a spot more on the hour throughout the day. Despite her alcoholic intake, or perhaps because of it, she was able to make a reasonable living from freelance journalism, even contriving to write satirical pieces on London social life from her Athens apartment. She was consistently unkind to her lovers, who never lasted more than a week or two. She would shout at them in public places; if one had really irritated her she would pick him up in a sort of fireman's hoist, sling him over her shoulder, and carry him down the street. I wondered now whether I even liked her, whether this visit might not be a wretched mistake. But beyond the drinking and ranting she was funny and generous and I admired the relish she took in her odd, lonely life.

The hospital was huge and parts of it were still being built. The hillside was gouged with quarry workings, and great grey bulldozers and cranes and diggers toiled slowly back and forth, changing places, revolving, realigning in a complex and enigmatic pavane. Dust thickened the air and clouded out the sky; the colour had leached from the landscape, leaving it lunar and featureless. A no place. I thought of the word *utopia* and its literal meaning of "no place" and how strange it is that this no place is always taken to be a desirable one.

Shining rivers of grey vinyl wound my way to Christina's room. I hesitated at the doorway, scanning the four beds. She wasn't there. Then "Hey, DUDE!" shrieked the weird person at the far end by the window. Christina was in disguise; she had dolled herself up as some kind of invalid country-and-western lady. Her hair hung down in blond ringlets, her décolleté night-dress bore a huge pink satin bow just beneath the bust, strongly suggestive of Easter eggs. Over it she wore a pink feather boa, wispily attached to a fluffy angora bed jacket. The boa flipped about, involving itself with a dangling tube hooked up to Christina's left arm. God, I thought, it's a blood transfusion. My Bloody Marys made a swift and shameful appearance in my mind; lined up on a silver tray, they reeled into darkness. "So what's the matter with you?" I demanded, sounding bossy and curt, cutting through Christina's babble about the *awesome* horror of hospital food. She was making me feel pedantic and English; she was making me hold tightly on to my handbag handles and sit with my feet in symmetrical parallel. "Nothing much"; she sipped some water or possibly vodka. "I had a pain in my stomach but it's gone now. They just won't let me out yet because they want to do some tests. Anyhow I'll lose some weight." I felt reassured by this non-reply and told her about a recent visit to an English casualty ward where I overheard a doctor interviewing a youth behind closed curtains.

Doctor: "So you have taken a number of tablets. Did you mean to kill yourself?"

Youth: "Dunno, maybe not really, don't know."

Doctor, keenly: "Ever thought of cutting your wrists?"

Youth: "No."

Doctor: "Do you have a garden shed?"

Youth: "What?"

Doctor: "A garden shed with weedkiller in it. Do you have access to weedkiller?"

Youth: "No. For goodness sake, what is this?"

Doctor: "Are there firearms in your house? In an unlocked cupboard?"

Youth: "Please go away. Just leave me alone."

Doctor: "So you haven't been tempted to shoot yourself?"

Youth: "Oh fuck off." He begins to sob.

Christina enjoyed this tale and laughed a lot. An eyelash detached itself and drifted down, iridescent and eddying in the late afternoon light. I remembered the harbour at Rethymnon and the kingfisher; it dipped back and forth among the boulders of the sea barrier, brilliant against a sullen, windy sky. Off it flew westward and all its colour was quenched into blackness before the pallid spot of the sun. The sea was swollen, pounding and dragging the shingle, the cafés were deserted, the tables stacked, the umbrellas furled. The melancholy of the changing season whined through the wind's skirmishes and the groan of the shifting shingle. All things are passing.

Christina was staring at me; I felt a pang of terror. Her eyes seemed to have receded into her skull; she gazed out as though from a cavern, withdrawn from the rest of the world, unreachable. And then she was back, complaining about the nurse who had confiscated her vodka bottle from her sponge bag, addressing her as Little Lady. "Bloody puritanical Yanks," she said. "I'd be better off in a Greek hospital. Anyhow I've a story to tell you too. I've been thinking about this a lot since I've been in here. Maybe it's the best thing that's happened to me; or maybe not the best, but the thing I've liked most."

Once upon a time Christina lived in Chicago. She was fourteen years old and her parents' marriage had just broken up, so that she and her mother had come from Texas to live with her grandmother. Christina hated it; she missed her old home and her father and her friends, and most of all she missed her ballet lessons. Her mother promised that when they were more settled she could take them up again, but Christina didn't believe her. Like everything else here, promises were nothing, air and water. Rudolf Nureyev had recently defected and was coming to dance in Chicago. They had promised tickets for this but of course nothing had been done and now there were no tickets left. She felt intense panic at the real facts of time passing and having nowhere to practise; she was getting taller every day and could soon be too tall to be allowed into ballet class. Or too fat, for she was bored and lonely and she ate too much. She seemed incapable of sitting down without having to eat simultaneously. Partly to avoid sitting down, and partly to make herself more miserable, after school each day she would walk for hours in the bitter late winter winds. Or was it early spring? The snow had gone, but the sky remained colourless, and the buildings were grey and the waters of the great lake were grey, whisked to a constant mean turmoil by the crazy, buffeting winds. Air, water, nothing, and noise, aircraft, sirens, traffic, foghorns, construction work, wind booming round the corners of the blocks.

So there Christina went, trudging along in her tight red woolly hat and her unmatching gloves, her winter trousers and boots. She dragged her soles along the concrete walkway by the lake, head down, doubled over against the roaring, idiot enemy. Her eyes stung and her chilblains itched. In the near distance a dark figure was moving rapidly, purposefully, towards her. A man. She peered round; there was no one else in sight. Her heart began to thump; God, she prayed, if you don't let him kill me, I'll stop going on these stupid walks. A flight of geese rose shrieking off the lake and passed in formation high above her, darkening the sky with omen. Their wings creaked as they went. Now the man confronted her; he stood still. Christina stood still. He wore a black cloak which puffed and billowed towards her, as if to envelop her. Speechless, she stared at him, and the breath caught in her throat. It was Nureyev. He swept off his floppy black cap and bowed in a deep curve of sinuous grace. Her eyes still fixed on his face, Christina sank into a curtsey. Their gloved hands clasped as he raised her to her feet. Then they walked on in their opposite directions. "And I didn't look back," Christina concluded, triumphant, glowing. But a moment later her eyelids drooped and the colour had faded from her cheeks. "I'm really sorry but I have to take a rest," she said. "I've had it." I thought then that she meant she was exhausted; perhaps she did. I kissed her goodbye and I went. "And I won't look back," I said.

She died that evening, but I didn't know this until I was home in London. I sat out then on my balcony in sultry October dusk and watched the planes stacking and sliding past the pinnacles of Westminster Cathedral and I thought of Christina and the crones and the dogs of Athens, sleeping by their own cathedral, littered in shaggy heaps about its glassy forecourt. I remembered a flower seller appearing in the early morning square, making his way round the café tables. In seconds the dogs were up and barking; they saw him off and returned to their slumbers. Later I saw them dispersed through the streets, sleeping again, by dark shop doorways. At the airport they were busy as before, seeking companionship with no great urgency, amiable and bright of eye. The three crones sat knitting in their row of chairs and one of them dropped the orange ball of wool. It rolled out across the floor and a sheepdog bounded towards it. I moved fast to intercept it but it had gone. I could not tell whether the dog had seized it, the woman had picked it up or someone had kicked it off under the chairs. In my head there was an image of a pomegranate rolling across mosaic tiles and a hand outstretched to catch it, the hand of a person unseen, something from a half-forgotten poem two thousand years old.

MOMENT OF TRUTH

Unedited interview with Colette Douglas-Home

All my life I loved poetry and longed to meet a poet. From the age of twelve on, I used to pray to the moon with tightly clasped hands and pray, "Bring me a poet." I had read George Barker's poetry before I met him and had that marvellous kind of thunderclap feeling—that "Wow . . . I love this!"—and the tingling spine. And then I did meet him.

I was about twenty-one, I think. I was living in Scotland at the time and had come down to London to see an old friend, Donald, who was in fact living in Rome and had met George there. George was also in London visiting Elizabeth Smart and his children and old friends. So we met up.

Donald took me over to meet George at Elizabeth's flat. I had met Elizabeth already two or three times and got on very well with her. George was not living with her, but staying with her. She had a huge rambling flat in Paddington and there was always room for him. He was living with another lady in Rome. That relationship was breaking up but I knew nothing about that at that time. He lived in Rome full stop.

And so we met and got extremely drunk. I think both of us drank whisky at Elizabeth's flat and George and I got on very badly indeed. Yes, well, I was rather straight-laced. He showed me his book called *The View from a Blind Eye*, which is in some ways the one I like least of his books. He showed me some poems that were meant to be funny and I didn't think they were funny and was drunk enough to say so. That caused such explosions of wrath. Nobody had ever been so rude to me ever and I was still young enough and Scottish enough, and, you know, well brought up to expect one was polite to one's elders and one's elders were polite back. I just couldn't believe it.

So anyway there was this massive bloody great row and the only odd thing about it was that Donald, who was with me, got fed up with me and went off to Chelsea, where we were staying, so there I was. George's son Sebastian said I could sleep on the floor of his bedroom, no strings attached or anything. So when, at last, clearing up the whisky glasses time came, I made my way up to Sebastian's bedroom and George uncharacteristically pursued me upstairs saying, "Where are you going?" I said Sebastian had said I could sleep on his floor and he said, "Oh no you don't." So he woke his daughter Rose up and forced her to get out a camp bed and even made some motions of pretending to help her make it up. I was to sleep in Rose's room.

And you know retrospectively I realise this was the most un-characteristic behaviour. I have never known George to do this. He never gave a damn where anyone slept. Well anyway, we met in some pub a few evenings later and I expected him to apologise to me which he didn't do. So in fact I cravenly apologised to him. I did think he might then bring himself to apologise to me but he just said, "I forgive you, my dear" and I thought, "You bastard."

I wasn't attracted to him at this stage. I thought his poetry was fantastic but he had been so volcanic and horrific there was nothing but a kind of shock still in me.

But then we started drinking and then we started talking and then we started laughing and then I realised, you know, there was a completely different side to him. I went back to Scotland and he came to visit me. There was no romance whatsoever, just talking, and a good deal more drinking, scandalising my father.

Then I went to London to try to seek my fortune all over again and fell in with another friend of George who was planning to go out to Italy to visit him. He asked if I would like to come along and he wrote to George saying is it all right to bring Elspeth and George sent a telegram back saying "Thank you for thinking of such a nice present."

So this chap Tony and I went out to Italy and Tony warned me against George all the way. George by then had split up with his wife in Rome. I call all his ladies wives because I think they deserve status. There is no other way to describe a serious relation-ship producing children, lasting many years. To say "that woman" or something is unfair, it's wrong and I dislike the word *partner*. I dislike it very much. *Mistress* is wrong too. It is too louche to describe a domestic situation, so I think *wife* will do fine. It may be unemancipated but *tant pis*.

So George was living in a most lovely cottage out in the Alban Hills near Lake Nemi of *The Golden Bough*, if you know James Frazer's *Golden Bough*; a fantastic sort of haunted place where the priest-king, the king that had to die, used to pace those woods. There was a great deal of ritual connected to it, the worship of Diana and this high priest known as the priest-king guarded the sacred grove until such time as somebody came to supplant him and he was murdered. He knew he had to die. It was a very strange haunted place; and guarding the golden bough with his sacred branch and a green volcanic lake where the Emperor Nero once kept his pleasure boat.

It was a most romantic place, wild chestnut woods, white violets, and in the summer wild strawberries, very delicate . . . elegant. So anyway, there we all were, going for long walks (again I have retrospectively discovered this was completely out of character with George) and talking about Horace and love of poetry and oh it was just absolutely heavenly. Tony was still there and then George got fed up and kicked him out and asked me to stay on; the romance having burgeoned by then. Actually it was the night Kennedy died. You know that classic "Where were you then?" Tony then came bursting in through the French windows into our bedroom shouting to me, "Get to your room." It was so funny I just started laughing. George shouted at him, "Get out of my house. Get out. Get out." Tony then dramatically went off with his easel and his paints and got the last tram into Rome; suddenly departed to a Greek island where he has remained ever since. There had been some rows before that. He had hoped to be a romantic partner. He tried to strangle me, in fact, in the sacred grove of Nemi, but having been brought up in a boys' prep school I was able to deal with that.

So then we continued to live in this marvellous cottage. There was an ancient contessa who was our landlady who lived in a villa at the top of the gardens, the huge garden grounds with mimosa trees coming into bloom. The scent of mimosa is very evocative of that time. And so we took off from there.

I did have some wild and dreadful thoughts about "Oh dear what will my parents say about all this?" I'd written some lies about acting as a personal assistant to this poet, well, they had met George before, under rather drunken circumstances. Then we wanted to have a baby and that was duly accomplished.

Marriage didn't bother me. It was only when I thought of my parents' reaction I thought, "Maybe I should be married. They will not like this." But it didn't bother me. I suppose I was on a headlong go-for-broke. I was aware of George's track record but I also had the ludicrous arrogance of youth, you know, "I can do it," and I also thought if I can't do it I shall destroy him in revenge for what he has done to other women. He didn't know that.

Fortunately the positive rather than the negative side developed so we eventually came back to England in time for the first baby to be born. Elizabeth would say he wasn't husband material and he wasn't really, but he was a fantastic father to all his children, adored all his children, and they get on very well with each other.

He was not good husband material because he was a poet. Poetry mattered more to him than anything else in life except possibly his children; so one was always really playing second string to the muse. It could be very trying. I am a very undomestic person and, you know, trying to cope with things like builders and coal and lighting fires and keeping the car taxed. He didn't do much. He drove. I mean he drove with great verve about the place but you had to do a lot of kind of bullying to get things kept remotely legal. It's not that one cares particularly about being legal but it is a bloody nuisance being caught, no tax, no MOT, etc., and bills have to be paid or the telephone is cut off. Little things like that. And if somebody is scribbling away and the milkman is beating on the door and they won't hand over a cheque . . .

At that time I had no money whatsoever. I was interested in babies, I wasn't interested in having a job. It was very self-indulgent of me. George adored them once they arrived. He was dubious every time I got pregnant. We didn't have little chats about "Let's have another baby." I just got on with it.

I suppose that meeting George totally and utterly changed my life irrevocably. We were together almost thirty years until he died last October, and it got better and better and better.

———————

George, despite the age gap, was completely ageless. He was just George. You wouldn't have thought, "Oh, he is seventy-eight," which he was when he died. You know, he used to like to say broodily in his cups, "Man is a spirit," and he was a spirit and I trust is a spirit and I feel his presence around a lot, not in a kind of fanciful way, but an overseeing power.

I suppose at first I was still very overawed by George as a poet, as aside from being George, and gradually you become accustomed to that. But poetry was the mainspring of our lives together. He always got me to read anything that he was writing and talk about it and so on. When we get drunk we always read poetry to each other. Drink is another important feature of my life. Saturday nights were drinking time, really. George was very disciplined about it. He could not work with a hangover because he always drank vast quantities and so he had to work during the week; but Saturday nights were massive drunken occasions. That was actually not too easy to handle when the children were small. We were trying to get them to go to bed and they would come down and there were always loads of people round and you were trying to cook them some filthy spaghetti or something. You can imagine. But of course the children get older and it all sorts out.

We couldn't get married before we did because George was married once when he was young. Initially when we came back to London after the first baby was born he did say "Let's get married," but we couldn't trace his first wife. She was somewhere in America. We did go to a lawyer and so on but he was just very incompetent and then after a bit it really didn't bother me.

My parents, after a bit of initial reluctance and crossness, accepted my dubious status and then eventually we did find out where his wife was. She was living in Kentucky in a kind of home and she had Alzheimer's disease and there was no way you could . . . it would have been very distasteful really and George was a Catholic as well. But she did die in the year we got married and we decided it would be a nice thing to do. It would be a sacrament. So it was just a sort of confirmation and a consecration of our time together. I thought it might be very nice for the children. But it had never occurred to the children that we were not married, so they were all very shocked. I think they thought it was quite funny.

In a way my upbringing all tended towards George. My parents had been so fond of poetry themselves and they had always encouraged us to learn by heart and so poetry was always threading a way into one's head anyway and so it was a right true end to it all even if it did break a few rules. For the future my writing and my children are the two things. I don't want to marry again. I have done that.

JEALOUSY

If the infant is primitive so is its earliest vice, jealousy—probably the most innate vice of all. First comes love, then jealousy, an unholy, uninvited symbiosis.

Once there was a great gaunt dog called Griselda, who lay, snarling softly, in an alcove beside the blacksmith's furnace. With clash and with clangour he shod Bonny and Beauty, colossal Clydesdales, and Griselda's yellow eyes narrowed and flickered in the spark light. One day she had a litter of squally pups. In the late afternoon, as darkness gathered and Mr. Gould shook the sweat from his hair and damped down his fires, she ate them. You could see she did not want them.

I told my mother and she said, "No, it was Mr. Gould's fault, they should not have been near all that noise and disturbance." That was clearly rubbish. If it were true, why had my mother not eaten her babies? I wanted her to eat them. I stumped about shouting. She smacked me hard. "Don't be ridiculous," she said. "What on earth's the matter with you? The trouble with you is that you have a nasty jealous nature."

How very true. I longed to be called Griselda, and it was with intense relish that I read the ballads of my native land. They have a swift way of dispensing with nuisance. "The elder came and pushed her in. / Sister o Sister, sink or swim" or the betrayed wife, Annie: "Gin my sons were seven rats / Rinnin oer the castle wall / And I mysel' a great grey cat / I soon would worry them all." My brother and I tried and failed to despatch one sister; for a while I considered losing others in the forest. It became obvious, not that it was wrong, but that there was no point. The world expanded and it contained greater attractions than self-laceration over siblings. Even so, the occasional frisson lingered. Contemplating a roast suckling pig in a wondrous shop in Soho, called, I think, King Bomba, I considered the possibility of my youngest sister served thus, with an apple in her mouth. I studied Euripides's *Medea* with an enthusiasm which contained nostalgia; how fine a dinner I might have offered to my parents. That would have shown them.

Jealousy, of course, should not be confused with envy. In the teen years one may yearn to have smooth blond hair or (as in those ancient days) a dirndl skirt or divan beds with matching candle-wick bedspreads, or a mother who wears white lipstick, but this is not the consumer, the passion, the "green-eyed monster which doth mock the meat it feeds on." The carrion beast slinks on scene again with boyfriends, husbands, or whatever one calls them. Although I have been mainly fortunate in avoiding its attentions I have experienced them and have become again a murderess. I have stood at the top of a flight of stairs ready to drop a stone cross on an unsuspecting but guilty head; only the presence of a baby against my shoulder stopped me. The monster's only joys are violent and transitory; but its poison is all-pervading and irreversible. It is no wonder that the jealous person's countenance is traditionally tinged with green. The only cure lies in oblivion.

Female jealousy is associated with witchery, bitchery, dementia, and underhand behaviour. Its manifestations are often inventive—the abbreviation of a chap's Armani suit or other bits, the share-out of his wine cellar, the mutilation of his motor. I know a woman who has taught her much younger husband's beloved parrot to address him in her voice, uttering sweet blandishments, offering evening drinks. "Just so he'll be sorry later, when he's with someone else."

Men seem more straightforward. They just kill the woman. You are doubtless aware, but it is worth repeating, that marriage or similar makes a woman 70 per cent more likely to meet a violent end, at the hands of himself. The word *zealous* and the word *jealous* have the same Ancient Greek origin signifying an eager rivalry, an uplifting admiration, a passion with nobility. Plato set it in opposition to envy or *phthonos*.

There is a handy old expression, *oudeis phthonos*, or as some still say, no sweat (man). Othello, literature's great jealous man, is constantly described as noble, even when behaving in a manner that is frankly ludicrous. After endless bombast and drivel over the missing handkerchief, he goes storming off. Emilia says percipiently: "Is not this man jealous?" Desdemona is stunned: "I ne'er saw this before. Sure there's some wonder in this handkerchief." The noble Moor then reappears: "Handkerchief—O Devil!" (falls in a trance). Later of course he says, "Wash me in steep-down gulfs of liquid fire," and therefore can be forgiven anything. Nonetheless, that cry of "Handkerchief" seems to me to share a little place in the great scheme with Lady Bracknell's "Handbag."

Personally, I eschew all that sort of thing these days and am more interested in trying to write a villanelle or discovering thirty useful things to do with radishes. The monster has shambled off over the hill, though sometimes I still see its shadow. Or not? Recently, I sat in a hospital bed, wearing a seductive hospital nightie, ashen-faced, hollow-eyed, drips and tubes tangled about me. Mad Bertha after fifty years in the grave. Someone I do not like remarked: "You're looking ten years younger." "How could she say that?" I screeched at my daughter. "Don't worry, she's just jealous," said the beguiling nymph.

When I was little I associated jealousy with jellyfish. I often encountered these creatures while swimming in the far-from-unpolluted waters of the North Sea. I have no intention of ever again setting foot in that icy ocean; nor shall I be jealous. Jealousy, jellyfish, see if I care. Or as one might say, lemon jelly, kiss my belly.

MEMORIES OF
GEORGE BARKER

Much of late has been written about George's wild, bad lifestyle, in reviews of Robert Fraser's biography, *The Chameleon Poet* (2001). Since when was it the business of a reviewer to moralise? If they had persevered to the end of this very long book, they might have noticed that for the last twenty-eight years of his life, George stayed in one place, with one family, a present and devoted father to our five children, who adored him then and now. It is not for me to criticise his earlier behaviour, nor will I deny that our time together was often turbulent. It was also vivid and passionate and treasured. To countervail that spiteful litany of blame, I offer a few glimpses of the George I knew.

Unsurprisingly, as the father of fifteen children, George loved babies; babies responded, eyes shining with delighted recognition and conspiratorial glee. Few men of his generation were happy, as he was, to push a pram, and entertain its occupant through the streets of London. "Babies are cherubimos," he would say. "They have wings." Before I met George I had never liked them one bit; he made me see things differently. The early morning tea ceremonial began the day in Norfolk. Panels of river light and leaves flickered on the bedroom walls; the five infants rolled and bounced about us. In the brass knobs at the far end of the bed our reflections were strangely curved and elongated, like the Henry Moore king and queen who sit alone and brooding on a Scottish hillside. Or a Saturday night memory: George as usual behaving badly, drunk, dangerous and belligerent, but at last, to everyone's relief, gone off upstairs, and someone realising that she'd left her six-week-old baby wrapped in her shawl on the bed. There they both lay in deep sleep, George saintly as an effigy, the baby moth-like clasped on his chest.

Saturday nights did have their good moments, before the ravening ghouls he observed in Robert Colquhoun came to taunt him in his turn. He would alarm and entertain visitors by his singing habits. Leaning on the drinking room mantelpiece he would grasp a vase and intone plangent cowboy songs or Thomas Moore's lyrics. Sometimes he played an invisible violin. At dinner people scrambled to sit next to him, to be out of his missile firing line. But when he chose to read poetry aloud, seldom his own, often Hopkins or Yeats, or the anonymous "Quia Amore Langueo," he held the room spellbound. Not everyone was a poetry lover, not everyone could cope with the badness and madness, but they would still turn up on Saturday nights.

During the week he didn't drink at all. His discipline was rigorous. Apart from hangover Sunday, he wrote every day, sequestered in his study. If he was going through a barren phase, he would still keep the pen moving, into prose or rude limericks about fellow poets. He kept his notebook with him at all times, and if it was full, would use the nearest book. Georgette Heyer was the only twentieth-century novelist he was prepared to read, and the house is scattered with curling paperbacks containing scatological overspills. The Muse came first among his women, and she was the only one to control him.

He had great enthusiasm for all forms of sport. Part of Saturday ritual involved the wrestling on television, Big Daddy and Giant Haystacks. The Grand National was for him the first day of spring, a joyous family sweepstake and an epic of courage and nobility. I thought, after he died, that if any occasion could bring him back, this one would. I held a solitary sweepstake, allocating horses and money, but it didn't work.

Cars were another obsession. He was a skilful but lawless driver; I would never go in the front with him, sitting instead behind, rigid with fear. Sometimes this made people take him for my handyman driver. In a few weeks he could reduce a perfectly viable car to wreckage, by inventive tinkering; baked bean cans, lawn mower plugs, and chewing gum played their part. He had some unusual ideas about motoring. "In fog always drive on the wrong side of the road." "Never change down at junctions." "Indicators are for women." Driving, like drinking, was to him a non-domestic activity, ideally separate from the rest of life. Sometimes we had two cars, and I would creep along in the death-trap reserved for women and children, while he swept about the countryside in something flash. He hated to part with a wrecked car and often the garden became a scrapyard. Even now his 1960 Mercedes Benz continues its disintegration in an open-sided shed, conspicuous and immovable.

When someone has died, it is tempting to see their manifestation in another form, a hare, moth, the shape of a cloud. For George I fancy the white owl, who at dawn shrieks defiance from the ridge of the roof to a parliament of owls heading home from hunting. And each autumn, in the churchyard, a solitary specimen of the brazen mushroom *Phallus impudicus* rears from his grave. That would amuse him.

CHERUBIM

It certainly isn't worth it, the day term begins and life is supposedly reverting to drab and normal.

The dawn light yet again reveals great muffled shapes, wearing boots, on every sofa. It is worse in the kitchen, where, the previous evening, I set the table with a keen eye to the assertion of Family Values (dinosaur mugs and blue stripy bowls) in the face of drunken revelry. Now there is a moraine of overflowing ashtrays, sodden cigarette packets, half-empty beer cans, spilt wine. I hurtle about the sofas, screeching. Nothing happens. In one room I plug in the Hoover and leave it turned on and roaring at the sleepers; in another I send the remote-control New York police car into action, siren wailing, horn blasting, lights flashing. There is a distant chatter of machine-gun fire. I fling open windows and hurl coats into the rainswept garden. I drop a few cats around. Silently the shapes rise, clear up the kitchen, retrieve their dripping coats from the puddles. The air is heavy with injured innocence, unspoken reproach.

I remember the hymn our headmistress thought appropriate for the first day of boarding school term: "Can a mother's tender care / Cease towards the child she bear? / Yes! She may forgetful be . . ." Oh God, I think. Soon they'll all be back in London, and then I'll miss them. I didn't really have to chuck their coats out. Suddenly I am exhausted, my heart begins to thump and guilt comes seeping in. One of them gives me a cup of tea, complete with sugar and milk. My heart brims with gratitude. Oh, happy is the mother whose child, unbidden, gives her a cup of tea. Third son used to say that he would look after me when I was old and mouldy. I am no longer the murderous harpy of ten minutes past; I am old and mouldy. Does he notice? I am a mental and physical wreck and it is all their doing. "They fuck you up, your mum and dad." Philip Larkin had it the wrong way round. Mind you, I'm glad he wasn't one of my children.

So where have they gone, the cherubim, the magical babes, each of them once the world's most beautiful? Sometimes I dream of them and wake in tears of loss and bereavement. And other sunderings follow. The time when their friends become more important than their parents; teen time; leaving home time. My fourteen-year-old daughter ceased to kiss me goodnight because of her great hatred for me. I knew a lot about this hatred because I used to read it up in her diary. But one evening she had a school friend staying. This friend embraced me warmly at retiring time; whereupon the hissing viper of my bosom followed suit and bade me goodnight with a breathtaking show of filial devotion. That Judas kiss caused me acute pain for a long time.

Much later, during a friendlier period, she returned from a holiday in Spain. I was very excited; she had never been away for so long. As I drove, fearfully and illegally, a great distance to collect her, I planned a happy mother-and-daughter evening, enhanced by a bottle of gin to indicate her new adult status. We'd been home for seven minutes when she was off with an unknown youth in a bright orange sports car. "Thanks for fetching me, Mum. I'll be really late, so don't stay up." I shared out the celebration meal between the cats and dogs. Then I drank the gin.

Boys torture their mothers in a different way. They do dangerous things and they often look very peculiar. One son decided his ears stuck out; he glued them to his head with superglue. He combed the woods for small dead creatures and simmered them in a great cauldron on the Aga so that he might extract their bones to make necklaces in the manner of the Plains Red Indians. He also threaded bones into his hair. His brother, pogo dancing, split his skull on a nail protruding from the ceiling, and had to be rushed to hospital. He was dressed as an Egyptian mummy and the cerecloths and bandages were very serviceable in soaking up the blood. Another fell off a motorbike and smashed his leg. Another ate a bumper packet of firelighters. I have spent a great deal of time hanging about hospitals, waiting for them to be mended.

At night I still lie awake, inventing accidents more improbable even than the ones which have occurred, on the quaint principle that if I've thought of them they won't happen. You are never safe again after you've had a baby, terror and loss lurk around every corner. You are perpetually alert, straining after the ghostly voices of children long grown, an infant crying in the night.

I would like to be one of those wooden Russian dolls and have them all packed neatly back inside. I am a non-PC mother, with matriarchal tendencies. It seems absurd that one should go through the mighty travail of rearing children, only to wave them goodbye. Buddy Holly sang that you might go your way and I go mine, his song title "It Doesn't Matter Anymore."

But they do matter, just as much as they did when they were little. And those babies, the cherubim, haven't really gone. Behind each adult child hovers a recession of all his or her earlier incarnations, like an inversion of the line of Banquo's unborn sons who appear at one of the cheerier moments in *Macbeth*, a jolly dinner party, I believe.

Contrary to ludicrous statistics, you don't need a lot of money to bring up children. You need persistence and guile, ruthlessness, resilience, and imagination. You will learn to bow gracefully to the inevitable (most of the time anyway) and you will become impervious to public humiliation. You must be able to laugh. And above all you must be able to love. All this they teach you. All this you owe to them, and in the end they owe you nothing. They are a privilege beyond accounting. Recently one of my sons won a bottle of Armagnac in a fancy dress competition; he was disguised as his mother. A dubious enterprise, but he gave the Armagnac to me. Definitely worth it.

APRIL

The countrywoman in the prolonged winter which is an East Anglian spring spends more time slithering on the public highways than straying down nature's byways. She apprehends the world through a mud-splattered windscreen. To some their Volvo, to others their Ford Cortina. While Volvo is a silly sort of name, meaning I roll something along, the Cortina is variously a cauldron, an Apollonian tripod, or, by poetic transference, the *vault of heaven*.

It's the one for me. Driving is not much fun round here because of the Highways Authority. Hospital wards are closed for lack of cash, little children are denied transport to school so that they, their mothers, and infant siblings are obliged to walk two miles there and back along roads pounded by juggernauts. For the mother this means a daily trek of eight miles but it's spend, spend, spend with the highways authority.

Where'er one roams, be it ever so remote, there they are with their traffic lights and their bollards and their bulldozers and their proliferating notices couched in highwayspeak: "Changed priorities ahead," they proclaim, and a few yards further on, "Cats eyes removed." What's in a priority after all? Oaks planted by Humphrey Repton have been felled and dragged away in chains. But one must feel for the tormented souls of these planners, if they don't spend all their money now they won't get any more next year. What a very pleasant arrangement.

It is pleasant, too, for the police, for they may lie in wait at the serial roadworks for the complacent motorist. Twice they have claimed they cannot see my tax disc. "Haha," saith the warhorse among the trumpets. There it is, dead centre of the windscreen, jammed into the middle of Kennedy's *Revised Latin Primer* and perfectly visible. It's bad enough to have to pay for a tax disc. But then to try to make it circular without tearing it, to spend a further 40p on one of those round containers which won't even stick to my windscreen, to insert disc into said round thing. *Non.* Kennedy is a comforting companion in the event of a breakdown. You may learn about the subjunctive of conditional futurity: *migrantes cernas*, "One would see them leaving" (if one were there).

"Lovely job," says the policeman, quashing disappointment. This sort of thing puts me in a bad mood when, eschewing the glittering wit of friends and family and the sullen charms of the Bulgarian vintage, I try to watch television. It is hard to rate this as an acceptable human pastime. The great god Car dominates the screen, there are the police again, then sex programmes and violence programmes. Only the two Clive men lighten the gloom, the hideous deadening vulgarity. And there has been the rugby which can be wildly exciting, an excitement enhanced for me by being in a warm room and remembering freezing afternoons at Murray-field, the only girl in the schoolboys' enclosure. With pigtails. My parents would not agree. They would like to be at Murrayfield, and they would re-create the sub-zero conditions in their well-ventilated morning room. There they sit in their coats and travel rugs, oblivious to all but the game.

The only other good thing about television is that recently, on separate occasions, two of my sons have appeared on it, one as an eighteenth-century footman, the other playing his guitar. A glimpse of Inspector Morse pretending to be Peter Mayle typing out of doors in the sunshine sends me in guilty retreat to my kitchen, where I try to write pulling my sleeves down over my numbed hands.

———

Yet day by day spring advances and the view from my bedroom window each morning is pure delight. At first in the overcast world of dawn the grass is dull and glaucous with dew. Then a great red sun lifts through the mist and clouded blackthorn blossom and the day dazzles. Budding branches blur the blue sky.

In the bronzing cherry tree immediately under my window sits a fat bastard pigeon gorging himself. I hurl my cup of tea at him; he continues to sit there. Now I have no tea; now I will have to get up. Proceeding to work in my Apollonian tripod I pass banks starry with stitchwort and celandine primroses, violets, cowslips.

How lovely it is to make lists of flowers. Virgil has some good ones in the *Georgics*, and Shakespeare in *A Winter's Tale*, but my favourites appear in Milton's *Lycidas*. I have been trying to collect these and I have come upon small, surprising difficulties. Last year I planted the white pink and the pansy freaked with jet, only to find that on a second blooming the white pink became a dingy pink pink and the pansy unfreaked, never to freak again.

And what of that sanguine flower, inscribed with woe, which I take to be the hyacinth, imprinted with the letters AI, the ancient Greek cry of agony, in memory of the cruel death of the youth Hyacinthus? Where are these letters? Try asking a garden centre that one.

The awakening of nature has its drawbacks too; I fear the presence of a hornet's nest, for on five recent occasions, gigantic specimens have been droning unsteadily about my bedroom, according special attention to the bedside lamp. One of them missed the lamp completely and subsided into my hair. It would not come out. I shook my head into the freezing darkness but to no avail. At last I was obliged to wander about the house like Lady Macbeth, wailing for help. There are those who don't care (*sunt qui*, plus generic subjunctive, suggests Kennedy) to be asked to capture hornets at two in the frosty morning.

Which brings me back to the kitchen, where, although Inspector Morse may be warm and the cats, moored like barges around the Aga, are warm, I am not. I stamp about on the ancient tiled floor, which is laid straight on the earth in the simple mode of our forefathers, and I consider the icy black underground lake which stretches beneath the house. I indulge in some active smoking. Cough cough, purr purr. Hoot goes the owl. Somewhere across the river a swan is softly sighing.

HENS I HAVE KNOWN

Literature, legend, and art honour the cock, potent symbol of masculinity, plumed and gleaming life force, harbinger of doom. Thrice he crew at Gethsemane and through the millennia his voice shrieks warning time and again:

> The cocks are crowing on merry middle earth.
> The channering worm doth chide . . .

And due homage has been paid to his pride, his arrogance, his colours, and his spurs. Not so the hen.

No need to dwell on the crass brutalities inflicted upon these creatures in the name of human greed. Hens dwell apart, invisible to all but their assassins, debeaked, desexed, suspended upside down on conveyor belts and finally beheaded to become pallid neo-natal objects known as "chickens," with no sentient past.

And so for most of us, our earliest intimations of the hen derive from ancient illustrations to nursery rhymes or, most especially, from the idyllic England of Victory jigsaw puzzles, a land of green and gold and blue, where rust-coloured rustic birds scratch comfortably about. How helpful they are, and how pleasingly their plumage tones with the aged bricks and tiles. "She lays eggs for gentlemen." This is her task.

Sometimes she deviates into motherhood, a wondrous sight, couched on her nest with a myriad little heads poking out of her feathers. But in this role she is not admired. "Mother hen" is a term of derision, implying pointless clucking, ungainly fussiness. Even to glorious Milton they are but "tame villatic fowls."

Well, mighty organ voice, I disagree, although I, too, once saw them only as a hospitable adjunct to the breakfast table, uneasily quelling a very early memory of a dog grinning ingratiatingly and wearing a large, bloody, and dead hen slung around its neck (a folk remedy for hen killing).

So hens came to us, and idyllic indeed were the early days; little children gathered dark brown eggs in straw-lined baskets, and sometimes, most magically, found a single stray egg laid among the ivy tendrils which smothered the oak tree's roots. But soon nature was out; hens let it be known that they were romantic, racist, cruel, heroic beings.

So many incidents, lives, deaths. There was the enchanting silkie bantam, clad in white Cossack trousers and matching tam-o'-shanter, who was so horribly persecuted by the rest of the flock (American puritans in sober black) that she fled and took up with a handsome cock pheasant. Over the stubble into the autumn sunset they strayed together, and in the spring she returned, with a following of shadow-coloured birds, a clutch of phantoms. Meanwhile those same puritans huddled malevolently along the kitchen dresser shelves, beady eyes fixed in triumph on the egg cups smashed below.

More noble is the memory of the tiny bantam Badminton (B is for Badminton, bird of the year) and her daughter Emerald, who died on their feet, wings outspread to shield their infants, in a terrible canine massacre.

Conversely, one heaven-sent summer morning, in the children's pond, the first tadpole had become an exquisite jewel of a frog, scarcely larger than a drop of water. But over the surface of the little pond came floating, mekon-like, a spider with a bubble-shaped air chamber and it stung the frog, who drifted lifeless and flattened in its eddy. Wild tears of grief and outrage; so, thirty-nine weeks pregnant and beyond belief rotund, I lay on the grass and stroked the tiny corpse with a fingertip. Astonishingly, it began to pulsate, feebly and then more strongly, until we were able to place it, gleaming and live again, on its rock in the water. A beldame hen strolled by and whipped it down her throat.

On a more tender level was the triumph of a hybrid bird, programmed never to reproduce, who managed to hatch a strange, damp, grey, long-necked creature of her own.

All our hens refused outright to live in their own run and consequently, over the years, having multiplied exceedingly, they formed three separate flocks, roosting with open scorn in the winter trees (bare ruin'd choirs where now the grim hens sit).

Many guerrilla raids were made upon the kitchen and on picnic rugs and tables, until we returned one weekend from a visit to a household not blessed with hens, and looking at our ravaged habitat decided: these birds must go. Forthwith they were rounded up for market.

All, that is, except for two cocks, a father and son, whom we couldn't catch, and one hen who emerged days later from a clump of catmint. And hereby hangs a tale for our times. For this hen's life now became a torment to her. Whenever she stopped to peck, a cock would leap vigorously onto her. Soon she would run when she saw them coming; but they ran faster. She became exhausted and emaciated, unable to eat or drink, to browse or rest. But the cocks, accustomed formerly to a vast harem apiece, were now inflamed with insatiable lust and had a fearful battle in which one slaughtered the other. Blood-boultered, a scarlet lacquer bird, he stood on his son's corpse and crowed.

And the hen continued to decline; her feathers fell out, bald patches appeared, her eye was dull, and her comb shrivelled. At the slightest sound or movement she was off. But one morning as she scuttled nervously across the grass, she paused, stretched her neck upwards, and she CROWED; this was not a crow in its full range of arpeggios, systole and diastole, but it was unmistakably a half-crow, and an intended crow.

On following days the crow grew louder and more authentic, until it was as richly resonant as Harvey the cock's own cry. And now her comb became pinkly elastic, upstanding, then red and splendidly serrated; her stubby tail feathers curved out in glossy black and green plumes. The hen had become a cock; perforce. So, no longer an anorexic concubine, nor yet a lustful rival cock, the metamorphosed and hastily renamed Hennery high-stepped it round the midnight house, crowing reproof to late-night revellers, anticipating dawn by many hours, accompanied and abetted by the former rapist Harvey. A prodigy indeed.

But from a dictionary of superstition, under the heading "Hen" a chilling warning came; if you have a hen which has changed into a cock you must destroy it at once, for it will bring death to your family.

Impossible to harm Hennery, but what a burden of knowledge, responsibility. Surely no one deliberately courts the Fates. The dilemma was resolved by the milkman who collided with the bird of woe one icy morning.

This story has oracular meanings which I cannot yet interpret. Late in the day as it is, therefore, I make my plea for the respect due to the magical, reckless, random, and august ovipositor.

PART 3

WIDOWHOOD

IN VAGLIAGLI

Long before I ever went to Tuscany, which was once Etruria, I saw in Rome the Etruscan Apollo of Veii, with his loving and pitiless smile. This was not the sun god of the Greeks or Romans: this god presided over human sacrifice. I understood him better after a summer in Vagliagli.

Vagliagli lies north of Siena in the hills, surrounded by steep, dense forest of scrub oak and pine. Above, narrow white dust tracks climb to a bare, lunar landscape. The people of Vagliagli are called the Vagliaglini; they are swarthy and inscrutable, they do not speak to strangers. For those who wish to be serious about wine there is a famous *enoteca* in the village, much frequented by Saxon plunderers. Their Volvos whirl in and out in clouds of dust. Otherwise it is a silent, lonely place. In late summer pregnant vipers hang from the forest trees of Vagliagli.

Below the forest line, on gentler slopes, are vineyards, and there, in a tall old house with thick walls, steep stairs, and tiny windows, overlooking a hamlet, we stayed one summer. Sitting in early evening on the terrace we watched land and sky merge into one darkness, lit only by a bell tower whose arched window became at last a glowing doorway into the black hillside; the air was fragrant with thyme and fennel, cicadas sang in the vineyard, and we felt blessed indeed. But the next day Patrick became ill, and day after day he grew worse, unable to eat, unable to cope with the stairs, suffocating in the infernal heat of a densely walled south-facing room. All the rooms in this house were hot. It seemed that the sun never really left it. Doctors came and went, reassuring, all specialists in heart and respiration; injections and drugs marked out the days' bright hours, impersonal and implicit with menace as the radials on a sundial, and bearing the sundial's urgent message, *Tempus fugit* and *Carpe diem*.

One night I sat outside to watch an eclipse of the moon. As the earth's shadow finally overcast it, I noticed that the rhythm of the cicadas had changed, slowing and labouring. I thought of Ecclesiastes, "And the sound of the grasshopper shall be a burden, For man goeth to his long home." The frail rim of light struggled, wavered against the engulfing blackness, burst out again in agonised pangs of sullen red, then suddenly was gone. The cicadas were silent. In panic I rushed up the stairs to our room. But he was alive, he was breathing steadily, and indeed the next day he seemed stronger and was able to come downstairs.

The house at this time contained many people, too many people, of the wrong age for each other. The two tiny children, worn out by the heat and unable to play on the thistly scrub outside, quarrelled and wailed unceasingly. Their intense pleasure was to feed the starving cats which slunk up the outside staircase into the living room. Soon fifteen starving cats were crouching behind sofas, leaping on tables, licking plates and saucepans, vomiting soundlessly on the cheerful rustic rugs. Two of them mated in the pot of basil. Fast as they were driven out by flailing adult arms, legs, and brooms, so fast they returned. Annie had a special cat, so stunted and emaciated that it lay limply on her lap or shoulder, doing no wrong, and passively enduring dolls' tea parties. She dressed it in a long baby gown and rocked it to sleep in a cradle, droning a tuneless lullaby. Later she found it there, stiff and dead in its pink-ribboned bonnet. The boys buried it, with difficulty, in the hard, dry melon patch. After that no one would eat the melons. The boys, too, were having troubles, missing other boys' company, but they were inarticulate in the face of the noisy competition from the little ones and the teenage girls. The girls wanted only to meet boys, older boys, Italian or British, no matter, so long as they were romantic and had transport. But there were only two of them, they spoke no Italian, and they didn't feel confident enough to travel the fourteen miles to Siena on their own. By day they slept, or seethed about the house, and each night, when the moon rose, they would put on their most beautiful dresses and run out into the vineyards, Titian hair and golden hair flying behind them, in search of an Endymion. But by daylight or by moonlight one man only walked along those white dust roads. He was the village priest; he had suffered a terrible and disabling illness; and was performing an autocure; between the hamlet and the next village and back again he trudged, his head askew, his twisted arms held strangely to the left, unable to speak, intent only on reaching his goal and starting out again.

Then there were ourselves, and our host and hostess, who gallantly maintained the idioms of a cheerful family holiday, with excursions and picnics, swimming and endless shopping and assurances that it was a joy to have us there, and no trouble at all to fetch drugs and doctors and have a sense of doom in the house. We drank a lot of wine.

On the day after the eclipse of the moon ("only for noctambules," proclaimed the local paper), we took Patrick and the wheelchair to Siena, to the cathedral and the marble floor of crazed Sibyls, Hermes Trismegistos, and the slaughtered Innocents. Among the votives hung five motorbike helmets. Patrick tried to reach the holy water in the great font by the entrance, dragging himself out of the chair, clutching the brim and sending showers out over other visitors. He could not see the stone fish lurking smoothly in its depths. Outside in the steep, hot streets, people stared at the wheelchair, and grotesque Fellini faces leered from shadowy doorways. Our economist host explained that Italy had achieved an economic miracle, *il sorpasso*, and no longer felt any need to be polite to foreign visitors. I pondered on the inscription over the cast archway in the city walls, which declares that Siena opens its heart to all who come. Siena keeps its sombre volcanic heart for its own. And rightly so.

Back at the house, exhaustion and anxiety were as usual pervading; the children had begun to quarrel again, when we were surprised by visitors, Jenny the faith healer and her psychotherapist husband, old friends of our friends. They were staying nearby. Jenny was a tall, fierce woman with wildly curling hair. She hated me on sight and I hated her, too. When she heard of Patrick's illness her angry features reassembled into an expression of possessive fervour. She must give him a Healing.

"Well, it's worth trying anything," I said wearily, incurring an X-ray blast from her cold, grey eyes, grey-green really, glaucous, probably the colour of the eyes of the disagreeable goddess Minerva, who was, I then remembered, the goddess of healing. Trying to improve our relations, I told her this. It didn't work; there had been no call for elitist and depraved classics in the schools of her childhood in bleak northern England. Up the stairs she went. After a few minutes I looked round the door; she was crouched over the bed, her hands hovering like pallid birds of prey over Patrick's stomach. She was muttering about blue being the colour of stress, she saw blue, she saw anger and fear. Tiny bottles were laid out in meticulous rows on the table. Patrick appeared to be asleep. When she came downstairs she told us that because of the gravity of his illness she had given him her special amethyst crystal. She had bought this in a shop devoted to the sale of crystals, and as she stood, waiting for the assistant, she had heard a high, constant ringing sound and all the crystals on all the shelves had beamed a great white light at her. I was longing for her to go because the doctor was due to arrive. She went, assuring us that she would be sending telepathic healing from her house to Patrick, and also, she added, to me.

That night, rain and wind swept down over the hills and sheet lightning exploded about the house. In the morning the skies had cleared and the sun again shone brilliantly. Patrick tried to get up, slipped, and fell heavily on the marble floor. Back in bed, he could scarcely speak, he could scarcely hear, let alone breathe. The doctor came again, with an electrocardiograph machine. As I watched the giddy peaks and troughs of his heart pattern, I noticed the amethyst crystal on the table, complacent and viscous as a jellyfish. I removed it to a drawer. Patrick had to go to hospital.

Hurtling in the ambulance down the white hill roads, pitted now and grooved with shining rivulets, my head was filled with monotonous refrains, "Will he live? Will he die?" over and over, banishing thought. Then, for the first time, I saw the hospital. Behind it, a perspective of distant hills, winding waters and towers, delicate as a quattrocento painting, and there, in the foreground, where once there would have been a crucifixion, a colossal structure of concrete blocks, united in a grid system, monstrous and shocking, but holding such hope as there was in the world. Where once there would have been a crucifixion.

———

Swing doors crashed, trolleys sped over acres of gleaming grey corridor, green-overalled doctors emerged, shouted instructions, vanished. The usual chaos of hospital admission wrought its usual despair. Patrick lay still, speechless and twisted on his stretcher, like one of the terrible contorted figures found in the streets of Pompeii. At last I was called to see the doctors. They sat in a row, young and glamorous, smoking and flirting with giggling nurses, behind a long table. There was nowhere for me to sit nor any suggestion that I should. I became aware that the insect bites which had turned my legs into swollen twin bolsters had burst and poison was trickling into my sandals. They went on smoking and giggling for a while, ignoring me. At last they spoke. Patrick was very ill. He should not have come to Italy. Why had we come to Italy? "Chiantishire," sneered one adventurous linguist. Useless to protest scorn and loathing of this expression and all that it stands for, useless to do anything but let them have their revenge on Englishness until they tired of it. I stood there meekly in my squelching sandals, a sacrificial heifer. And soon, indeed, they relented. Patrick had a fair chance of recovery; they would take good care of him. He could now go to his ward.

Many hours later, leaving Patrick in his bed, wonderfully restored to life, able to speak, hear, even laugh, and surrounded by kind and courteous older doctors, we went to dinner in a small restaurant a couple of miles from the house. The telephone rang. We sat rigid with fear, and, sure enough, the waiter came straight to us. But it was not the hospital. There had been a fire in the house, we must come at once. In the hamlet all the old people had emerged from their houses, the cats were crouched like a Greek chorus at the foot of the outside staircase, and the children, huddled in blankets, were weeping in the street. Everyone was safe, but inside the house there was a dense miasma so suffocating that you could only rush straight out again into the sweet night air. Earlier, the little children had gone to bed as usual with their windows and shutters closed against the insects.

They had a dim lamp in their room but tonight they complained it was too bright, although they would not have it switched off, so one of the boys had propped a large floor cushion against it as an improvised shade, not, of course, touching the bulb. Hours later he had by chance gone upstairs and smelt terrible fumes coming from the babies' room. They were sound asleep, the cushion was blazing, the floor was smouldering, and thick smoke, pungent and murderous, billowed out as he opened the door. Too choked to shout for help, he had pulled the shutters apart, dragged the windows open, and hurled the foam-stuffed cushion into the street, blindly stamped his way through the flames to the little ones' bed, and pulled them down the stairs. The others beat out the burning mats. So they were safe, but nearly not. That night, when at last the fumes had dispersed, we slept, or tried to sleep, with every window open, and the mosquitoes and hornets and phosphorescent beetles joined the cats in wild marauding and no one cared.

Meanwhile in the hospital Patrick had been taken off his drip and settled for the night. He woke in darkness knowing that he was in a South African prison camp. Stark naked, this man who had been unable to move only a few hours before leapt out of bed and fled from the ward, pursued by Hassan, the Iranian in the opposite bed. Hassan had pneumonia. Down the silent corridors they sped, past the night nurse, who was dozing; Patrick shot into the lift, leaving Hassan clutching at the blank doors; he found another ward and took a shower, then, dripping wet and skidding perilously on the grey linoleum, he neatly skirted a prison guard advancing with a syringe and bolted again out of sight. From ten at night until five in the morning he maintained his mad career around the hospital, visiting among many places the ophthalmic ward, the spare mattress warehouse, a deserted cafeteria, and finally an operating theatre where he was captured by astonished surgeons. High rails were placed about his bed, but these proved no obstacle to the chameleon poet: he vaulted lightly over them; this time, though, he could go no further than the ward doors. The day staff had come on duty.

So it was that when we came to visit him, the three others in his room were laid out flat in deep sleep. He himself was both frightened and exhilarated by his adventures and claimed to be looking forward to the next night. However, for the next night and a couple after, I stayed there with him in a bizarre reclining chair and these nights were without incident. I say without incident, but I will not forget the restlessness and palpable fear which accumulated in the very early mornings, in the hours before dawn, when the old men would whisper and call out to each other to make sure they were still alive; and then they dared not sleep in case the darkness took them. When the sun rose there was such joy. "Allah has brought us another day," said Hassan, beaming. And they would prop themselves up and gaze out at the towers and the far hills and the cypresses still scarved in mist beneath the green, translucent sky.

───────────

Patrick grew stronger and the days assumed their own slow rhythm in the world outside a world that is a hospital. I read to him and I read the Italian newspapers. At first, I could only cope with local news, the Palio and the polecats which were wantonly ravaging a village near Vagliagli. "A new ecological disaster" and "*Paura nelle Case*." They hurtled from rooftops and they had consumed a Persian cat and a Pekinese dog. Becoming more ambitious, I studied a photograph of a monstrous fish like a squashed banana skin with a skull's face; it had been found in Cornuvaglia, perhaps another outpost of Vagliagli, pullulating with vitiated nature; in fact it turned out to be Cornwall. But as in Britain, so in Italy the greater horrors were the human ones. Immigrant Black labourers were being subjected to conditions of the utmost squalor and brutality and then viciously murdered as they worked on the tomato harvest. I thought of all those cheerful blue-and-red tins of tomatoes that brighten the murk of British country kitchens with their suggestion of honest toil and laughter under a cloudless sky where the benign sun confers natural goodness. And the Camorra had been busy, gunning down little girls whom they had mistaken for middle-aged Mafiosi.

One evening when I returned from the hospital we went to dinner with Jenny the healer and her psychotherapist husband. I didn't want to go, but I was told that this was very rude, in view of her intense interest in Patrick's health and her continual sending of telepathic healing. So off we went up the moonlit trails, beneath the viper-garlanded branches. A thin fox slunk across the car headlights and a small owl glared malignly from a rotted stump. It reminded me again of Minerva, and her constant companion, the very little owl.

The house was huge, square and sinister, full of Chirico archways and airport-style furniture hand-crafted by its owner, a Dutch museum curator. The electricity quivered and quavered but didn't go out. It was costing Jenny, her husband, and two other friends two thousand pounds a week. But then there was a swimming pool, albeit quarter of a mile away and in the viperous woods. We sat for a few minutes on the terrace over a single glass of wine before we were driven indoors by a new variety of droning, devouring insect. In the dining room, one more glass of wine was poured, then the bottle we had brought was corked and put aside.

As we masticated our red cabbage with apple, and mushrooms with pistachios and minimalist pork, I asked Jenny whether she had met any pregnant vipers doing hydrotherapy in her pool. There was a small silence about the table while she dismissed this with a glaucous glance and a magisterial wave of the hand, turning in intense communion to her neighbour. Chastened, I ate my pudding silently, longing for another drink. Suddenly, Jenny's friend Sue was hugging me. "I feel so sad for you," she said. Well, I thought things weren't good, but they could be worse; however, in this world one must be glad of anything affectionate and so I hugged her back. A moment later things definitely improved. A stout bottle of brandy appeared on the table, accompanied by a tray of tea. We sat in our neo-Bauhaus chairs round a modestly smouldering fire. Talk turned to education, then to the middle-class ethic of postponed pleasure, then to how much danger children should be allowed. At this point, I remembered that in *Il Messaggero* at the hospital that morning, I had read of the sudden death of the famous psychotherapist R. D. Laing. Knowing that they only read several days' old copies of English newspapers, and thinking it might be a topic of mild interest, at a pause in the theme of whether or not to let children climb trees, I said casually, "By the way, did you see that R. D. Laing has died?" There was silence, so I added, "Yesterday, in the south of France, a heart attack." More silence. "Aged sixty-one, I think." The silence ended. Five people were on their feet shrieking, wailing, embracing. Jenny was foremost. "To have heard it like that! From someone like that!" she yelled, burying her head in her husband's black leather bosom. Then, advancing to the table, hieratic and deadly, she seized the brandy bottle and hurled it on the fire. A bolt of lightning ascended to the heavens. "Goodbye, Ronnie!" she cried. "Goodbye, Ronnie!" echoed the others. I noticed there were a great many black grasshoppers with red spots on their backs leaping about our feet and even onto the rows of empty airport chairs beyond the mezzanine. It was time to go.

A few days later Patrick left the hospital. We cried as we said goodbye to his three roommates. We cried and they cried and we all embraced again and again. "*Tanti auguri, tanti auguri!*" they called as we set off down that grey gleaming corridor. They stood in the room doorway, waving and smiling, and they reminded me of the souls on the bank of the Styx, stretching out their hands in longing for that further shore. Outside the hospital the sun beat down again, astonishingly brilliant. I knew then that the sun god of Tuscany is not the Greek Apollo, not the Roman Phoebus Apollo, but the Etruscan Apollo of Veii with his warm and pitiless smile. It was autumn then in Vagliagli. The hunters had gone and the birdless woods were silent. Small vipers slipped from the trees to burrow and nest in the soil of ancient Etruria.

THE LONGEST GOODBYE

It is a year now since my husband died. On the day he most hated, when the clocks turn back and our days pitch into cold and darkness. It seems like yesterday. Everything that has happened since is like an incident recorded in the chapter summary of an old history book, remote events impinging on someone else, seen through the wrong end of a telescope, the print almost too small to read.

My daughter and I sat in the registrar's office, eyeing a Thank You For Not Smoking sign. The kindly lady behind the desk handed out Benson & Hedges. "My boss said someone to do with a poet would be coming in," she told us. "He'll be sorry to miss you. We haven't had a poet before." The window looked out on nothing but stormy sea and sky, both the colour of muddy milk. Beyond the horizon was more featureless horizon, mile upon mile of freezing wind and water stretching on until the Arctic Circle. It was the right place to be that afternoon and I would have liked to have stayed there.

Moving about was peculiarly difficult; the days seemed endless. One step at a time, one hour at a time. None of us could eat; we drank a great deal and we had no hangovers. The evenings were almost bearable, when we sat round the fire and talked about George and laughed. Mornings were dreadful, each day renewing the knowledge of loss; but they also brought sheaves of letters, extraordinary and unexpectedly moving. To read anything longer than a letter was impossible; it was weeks before I managed to go through the obituaries, months before I was able to write. At first I shook a lot; I still do sometimes. I don't know why. It is not *timor mortis*. But I have been afraid of grief, afraid of drowning in it.

Even in those first numb days, there were moments of inadvertent mirth. There was the fund-raising letter from the Samaritans which arrived the day after George's death—"Dear Mr. Barker, Have you ever felt you couldn't last one more day?"—then the early morning call from the undertakers, intercepted by our daughter Raffaella, as she spooned porridge into her baby. "Sorry to disturb you, Mrs. Raffy Elly. We just wanted to know if you'd like your dad's grave dug extra deep? So your mum can go in too." Such moments smoothed a little time away.

Going back to work was weird and alien. I felt ill when I was away from home, except when exploring derelict mansions at sunset—a pastime provided by house-hunting relatives. The cold red sky, the rooks calling through ebbing light in unfamiliar terrain, the knowledge that another day was almost over were oddly cheering, a small respite.

I am aware that I am fortunate in being part of a large family but the state of grief is essentially solitary. Talking to friends who have been bereaved helps a little, but only a little. There are numerous well-intentioned books dealing with every aspect of loss. Jeannette Kupfermann writes movingly and courageously of her experience of widowhood in *When the Crying's Done* (Robson Books), but in the end it does remain her experience. Bel Mooney has brought out *Perspectives for Living* (John Murray), a collection of interviews with bereaved people; it makes for harrowing reading. While I can only admire the strength and goodness of the human spirit which illuminates its dark pages, I was left feeling horribly distressed and somewhat voyeuristic. A few common needs emerge: for ritual, for talk with others in similar circumstances, for physical warmth, for dreams of the deceased. Much more apparent is the unique nature of each person's grief. There is no assuaging, unless it be brought by time. This I have yet to see.

I find death absolutely unacceptable and I cannot come to terms with it. I can no more conceive of utter extinction, of never, than I can conceive of infinity. I cannot believe that all that passion, wit, eloquence, and rage can be deleted by something so vulgar as the heart stopping. Where have they gone? As I see it, there are only two possibilities: that the spirit exists in some other plane of being, with no relation to our living selves, or that the spirit exists on some level that is still connected with us. Naturally I prefer the second idea. To say I believe it is too strong a statement; but I wish to live as though it were so. I am not a widow, I am George's wife.

Why must our marriage be nullified by his death? Sons, daughters, aunts, friends all retain their relationship. I shall retain mine.

But *O the heavy loss now thou art gone*. When a lover, husband, or wife dies, the survivor has also lost his or her own self, the self that was refracted and reflected by the other, and all their shared and private past. No dialogue, no jokes. And what of the dead person's belongings, objects that mattered to him, objects from his earlier past? It seems to me a denial of his existence to dispose of them or lock them away. I am not making a shrine of these things. I simply feel that they have rights. Possibly, of course, I am off my head.

Be that as it may, the living spirit pushes up through the stone carapace of grief like tendrils of convolvulus and one composes one's own small survival rituals in honour of the departed. Each to their own. Mostly I watch the dawn; I am waiting for a time when I feel that I can look forward to the day. For now, the past is what matters.

BROKEN HEARTED

This is a grey north country morning, still and soft, a harbinger of the changing season, heavy with melancholy. In the little wood doves begin to call, tentative then dazzling in urgency; other doves respond; they repeat the notes over and over until all the air is clamorous, sobbing and calling and crying.

Beyond the trees the steep harvest land sweeps to the sky in a perfect curve of tarnished gold. "Don't do it, don't do it," warn the doves, sharp with anguish; and the sorrowing choral resumes: "I mourn for my love, I'll be chief mourner."

In this quiet place one rainy afternoon five hundred years ago, 13,000 men spent two and a half hours hacking each other to death. This was the Battle of Flodden; it destroyed the entire ruling class of Scotland and their king, gained nothing for either side, and need not have taken place. But, like the First World War, it left an aftermath of inconsolable grief, generations of widows and spinsters who remained bound to those men they had lost and not only could not, but would not, replace.

I remember them well from school days, those unmarried dedicated teachers, and I remember, too, our hideous unkindness when we spoke of them, for we assumed that no one wanted to marry them and this appalling state of affairs was entirely their own fault. Consider that hand-knitted magenta jumper, that bristling mole, that steely glare. Consider instead the broken heart, and the silent gallantry of its bearer.

One of the characteristics of the broken heart is silence. No talk may cure it, no therapeutic chat. Hans Andersen's Little Mermaid was dumb throughout her suffering. Dido's wound of loss sat deep and silent in her heart; only when she transfixed herself with her false lover's sword and moved metaphor into reality did the heart cry out. Sorrow drains the world of its colour. Dido's last time of happiness, as she rode out to hunt with Aeneas, glows with sunshine and gold and purple. After that there is only monotone and darkness. Tennyson, in passionate grief for Arthur Hallam, abandons his customary richness of sound and image for a language that is bleak as pain:

> He is not here. But far away
> The noise of life begins again
> And ghastly through the drizzling rain
> On the bald street breaks the blank day.

The idea of the broken heart is not itself peculiar to a romantic tradition, although other cultures have placed the seat of the emotions elsewhere, in the head or even in the solar plexus. But one must be careful to distinguish stylised stylish suffering from the genuine article, for it is confusingly entwined with Pre-Raphaelite attitudinising, and with memory, distance, and death.

Absinthe drinkers and wan lovers may be pale and wretched from obsession but not from irreparable internal invisible damage. Even now the state may be recognised; certainly in my childhood people still talked of dying of a broken heart, a condition both pitiful and virtuous; so in fairy stories and myths the victims of the broken heart may pass through tribulations to redemption, but not to reinstated happiness.

Five years ago my husband died. I am still not used to his absence. I still can't accept the fact of death, the notion that one must come to terms with it. How? It is an outrage, a violation of all our day-to-day precepts. We live as though it were not so; then suddenly it happens and life is irredeemably altered. And one's head is screwed round to a different angle, a new way of looking.

I remember a hospital ward in Siena; an elderly man had just died, propped on his pillows. Across his chest his widow lay screaming: "Where are you? Tell me where you are." The other inmates went on eating their lunch and reading their newspapers and through the window the August sun poured down. Where are they indeed? And why, with all that time now available, should they not make a few brief appearances just now and then? Dreams aren't good enough.

I find that there are two kinds of dream. In some, life with the dead is as it used to be, pre-mortem, vivid and turbulent and funny and real. One wakes then into the renewed and shocking gulf of bereavement and it will not be a good day. But are these visitations or are they simply delusive memories? I must cling to the fancy of a visitation, however painful it may be to waken. Then there are the other dreams; it has all been a terrible mistake. He didn't die at all but we went and buried him and now he isn't in a very good state but he is back or coming back and the house is full of people who will put him in a rage, and *what has happened to his car?* "Considering you've been dead for five years you're looking really great," I babble, untruthful and placatory. This is all anger and guilt and nightmare and I wake, appalled to find that I am relieved that he is dead after all. So what's all that about?

There are daytime confusions too. A huge beech tree stands in my garden. We buried my husband beneath an identical one up in the village churchyard, a beautiful situation, shaded in summer and nobly rampageous in the winter gales. Beside the grave there is a tiny mousehole, and in the evening miner bees return from their labours and go processing in, two by two, underground. Their decorum is broken only by the occasional foray to sting my dogs. They ignore me. It is soothing to sit there on the bank and watch the bees and consider mortality and my own ultimate inhumation in this spot.

Down the hill, I can hear the voices of our grandchildren as they play in the stream. This year, in February, on a white morning still and cold as death, there came a crack of a rifle from the churchyard. The great tree had split from its roots and lay spread-eagled over the graves. Not a single stone was displaced; the branches encircled, caressed, bypassed every one of them. Beside the colossal trunk on my husband's grave, a glass of snowdrops remained upright and intact.

And within the trunk another swarm of bees was hibernating. Honeycomb dripped down its fatal hollow vault. People tried to save the bees but they died, of shock, of cold, who knows? But this summer, for the first time ever the beech tree in my garden has been loud, day in and day out, with a swarm of bees. Do the dead send coded messages or is one just a neurotic wreck?

Without that defining person in one's life, one is cast off balance, seeking a new identity. I certainly don't want to find myself, having spent half a century avoiding any such thing, but I need some point of fixity. That sense of being alone on a wide, wide sea is disquieting. It makes me dizzy. The evenings are very long. Sometimes it seems to me that there is no evidence now of those thirty years of shared past; they might have never been.

I heave out the photographs, I look at the photographs for a long time and I drink a lot. Once I read all of Shakespeare's sonnets to the photographs, once I and absence conducted a sweepstake on the Grand National together. I was obliged to take the winnings.

I am told we are expected to let go of the dead; what if the dead wouldn't want us to let go of them? Or do their wishes cease to matter, let alone one's own? Have they any idea of what we might be getting up to? I cannot yet believe that all that passion and wit and knowledge and rage can be obliterated by the failure of the beating heart. There are so many questions which seem unanswerable, set aside behind the spurious smokescreen called Coming to Terms with Death.

The word *widow* derives from the Latin *viduus*, empty; the drained vessel, the barren gourd. Great. It is a peculiarly colourless word with few and depressing associations; widow spider, Widow Twankey, that weird-looking young woman in a sort of mantilla advertising an insurance company equally weirdly called Scottish Widows. Or the widow bird who sat mourning for her mate. While the married state is undoubtedly preferable, I find myself doomed to solitude, monogamous beyond the grave.

It pains me when people suggest that after five years one might be forming new relationships; it seems cruel and disloyal. At first I could not enjoy anything at all; I also felt that I had no right to enjoy anything. This at least has passed. But I am aware of an abiding loss which qualifies everything I do and at times is overwhelming.

Certain landscapes, scents, and sounds, the lighting of the fire on a winter evening, a collection of boxes containing pen nibs and old clock parts and coins, can all without warning reform and metamorphose into Hokusai's towering glassy wave, suspended over the simple concourse of survival, the great doom's image. How could a heart not be broken?

PART 4

NEW
CHAPTER
OF
LIFE

THOUGHTS IN A GARDEN

Mine is a riverine garden, and even indoors one is aware of this, not just by gazing through the window but by simply sitting still, committing words to paper in intense cold, while a great numbness seeps up through feet and lower limbs. Hemlock and the death of Socrates come forward in the mind. The tiled floor is laid straight on the earth in the manner of seventeenth-century folk, and beneath this floor and a thin layer of earth lie the black sullen waters of an underground lake. This is true; I have seen those waters gleaming beneath a hole in the drawing room floor. Once the garden was fenland, embracing a much wider river, and Norsemen laboured up it in their longboats from the coast, intent on plunder and rapine. I am glad to have missed that.

Now time has modified the riverbank, where bramble and hawthorn and snowberry and ivy tangle to forestall small children from a watery demise, and a high beech hedge divides it from the lawn's long slope. This hedge is a source of anger and grievance in postmen, rubbish men, delivery men of all sorts; they claim that its tentacular outreach damages their vehicles, already woefully menaced by the muddy causeway which curves beside it, and mostly they refuse to come to the house. Which is fine by me, as I don't want to see them anyhow, except for the oil delivery man, who makes a ridiculous point of driving his colossal tanker backwards up the track.

Wet wet wet is the texture of the lawn, currently mounded by molehills of ever more ambitious scale. Wetter still is the stretch of wilderness leading to the pond and the graveyard of the important animals. Bog grasses are growing now, where once in more clement times my children played football or tried to hoist a sequence of angry ponies over jumps. I always chose the highest ground for the graves and I believe these noble beasts still sleep sound and dry; but even in the less sodden past the largest animal you could bury there would be a Labrador. Any deeper and it was standing water. Consequently, forty-one years on, space for final resting places is at a premium, and certain lesser creatures have had to be consigned to the edges of the lawn and peripheral nettly groves. Desdemona, the cat without character, lies here, and quite a few hens. I well recall beginning a new flowerbed and exhuming a dreadful pair of yellow legs complete with claws. "That's Joanna," observed a passing child, unmoved. Sombre, the trees gather about the upper graves, but in late winter their darkness is offset most exquisitely by the floating wanness of narcissi, and then wild primroses.

When we came here, all those years ago, the garden had ceased to exist. Nettles and brambles and ground elder and cow parsley and dock revelled luxuriantly through our first springtime. I had three children under three and was thus preoccupied; soon I had two more. My husband wrote his poetry in an upper room, looking out into trees, sky, and river, happily removed from earthly concerns. When summer at last came we began to reclaim the lawn. Children need grass and trees first of all. Then their animals needed grass, and the hens, disdaining their run, claimed the trees. Albertine and Madame Alfred Carrière clambered cautiously up the house and early morning light, refracted from the river, flickered and shifted through shadowing rose leaves down our red bedroom walls and danced in the brass knobs of the bed. Albertine was vigorous and gorgeously pink but died abruptly after only three years. Madame Alfred, however, continues to thrive and even this December displayed a scatter of ghostly blooms, whirled to the sky's four quarters by the bitter Norfolk wind. And as the years have passed, at last there is the time and chance to give attention to the flowerbeds, time to alleviate the whelm of greenery.

My husband, the poet, died some years ago and I have tried to make a six-foot garden on his grave; a rowan tree shades his stone and chequered fritillaries nod amid a profusion of forget-me-nots and foxgloves. In autumn there come the flaming arches of *Crocosmia*. But the garden for the living is another matter. I am blessed in having married again, and my husband, although eccentric and American, is a visionary gardener. I have seen him coax a rose, blighted and shrunk through wet and cold, furled tight in deathly pallor, into a perfumed ecstasy of splayed crimson, a performance so charged with eroticism that words must fail me. He has made a vast, overbalancing *Buddleia* into an airy cavern of blue delight, underplanted by cranesbill and *Campanula*; butterflies fold their wings along the silvery boughs and its haunting raspberry fragrance hangs in the air. I take intense pleasure in clambering up inside it and deadheading. There is an unearthly hush about the slow, gentle drift of the spent blooms to the ground, and through the branches I can see birds cross the wide sky, sometimes a swan, or a heron, or a flock of squabbling starlings, and I feel ethereal. But in truth I am a gardener manquée; I participate eagerly in the effect but do little to further the cause. Mostly I have the no-brain jobs, a little basic weeding, the wheelbarrow trundle to the unlightable bonfire, the gingerly poke at the compost heap. I am happy with these simple tasks; I believe myself useful but am without responsibility. Meanwhile, the paragon or paramour creates fabulous small vistas of colour, bells and spires; Saki's "bewildering fragment of fairyland" glimmers in sudden surprise as you wander past a shrub or around a tree. Look, look, we cry.

He is, however, obsessed with turnips. He grows them everywhere, among cornflowers, and tulips, and beside the miraculous violet sculpture of sea holly. Where'er your glance may linger, there rears a turnip. No other plant behaves like this. At all seasons they are conspicuous, in leaf, in flower, in white globular roots within whose deep recesses reptiles dwell. There are kindred disruptive elements in this garden; besides the molehills, a number of spiky dead trees present their barren limbs like amputees; still, they give pleasure to woodpeckers. Then there is the oil tank, behind which the junior dog has made a den, furnished by herself with stolen red cushions and Somerfield packaging; and we have the pathetic relic of the duck pen, containing an improvised and unused duck shelter fashioned from an abandoned azure plasterboard bookcase. Those ducks betrayed us. They sold us down the river.

Yet we can tell each other that the garden is beautiful, as the low white mist rises from the river and scarves the trees and we hear the sigh and rush of moving water, the toss of aspen leaves. The rainy-sounding aspens, Sappho called them, nearly three thousand years ago; the same sound now. And other people tell us that the garden is beautiful as they sit round the lawn table beneath the ancient beech tree. For those summer moments none of us will notice that the great tree is dying from its crown; indeed, to save its life, it is to be pollarded this very month, cut across in half. I absolutely cannot bear to think of this, but I can see that it doesn't want to die. It has already put forth buds for spring and beneath its bark three new trunks are rising from its roots; slim and shining grey, they press with youthful urgency into the aged soft white wood.

At the bleak time of year how tempting it is to lie in bed, cosseted like bulbs; we are aware of the dawn beyond closed curtains and we may consider the virtue of "maintaining a constant temperature in a dark place," as recommended so cordially by gardeners and oenophiles. But then, like bulbs and bottles, we must be brought into the light. A garden is idea as much as it is terrain, and now it confers perhaps its greatest blessing: the knowledge that whatever has happened, here we have another chance. Here there will be renaissance. In a garden it is never too late.

FRIENDLY FIRE

"*There is a shift in the wind.*" Oracular utterance, betokening woe. It was brought regularly by a kilted runner to my mother in her tower, from the far and dark recesses of the kitchen, the very shrine of the Aga, the household god, and its grim priestess, Cook. My mother would wring her hands and commence her customary smooth-running six-minute speech which treated with the injustice, inconstancy, and rigour of a life passed largely in an abnormal house, a vast stone castle crowned by battlements toppled regularly by this same wind, whose dominance extended even to the provision of life's basic necessities. A shift in the wind meant that the Aga was dormant; it meant that dinner would be late, or that dinner would not happen. Good news, however, for us children, cosy by the nursery fire and looking forward to a supper of Heinz Tomato Soup (sometimes Celery) heated on Nanny's Primus stove. Sometimes a jackdaw would provide diversion by crashing down the chimney into the fire, always to be saved, messily and energetically, by my brother. Otherwise this was a peaceful time, with the wind soughing and sighing through the pine trees far below and our mother's militant voice fading into the downward maze which led to the kitchen.

Even better if the wind was wayward still in the morning. These days people speak highly of porridge, cooked slowly, all night long, in an Aga. Ha! Year in, year out, there it was on the breakfast table, a grey, lumpy quagmire, every spoonful to be eaten up, impossible to flick under the table to a helpful dog. Lucky the little ones at their Midlothian Oat Food in the nursery. I wondered often if the porridge was kept in a zinc-lined drawer in great rectangular slabs for daily reheating, as in Stevenson's *Kidnapped*, but this I could never confirm, for children were not welcome in that kitchen. Nor was our mother, come to that.

It was a long, pale blue room, with a vaulted ceiling and a flagstone floor. A plain wooden table stretched from one end to the other, where the mighty triple-width Aga reigned from its raised dais. On the hot plates Aga kettles boiled continuously so that the air was hazed and steamy, and through the steam you might glimpse the white-clad forms of the irascible Cook and her acolytes, red of face, mighty of forearm. On the wall, usually askew, hung a Bateman print, "Cook Doesn't Feel Like It," depicting a drunken cook with her feet up on the table and an empty bottle rolling floorwards. But there were worse sights in the real and sober kitchen; bald, earless rabbits lay soaking in bowls of blood-tinged salted water, or brains or sweetbreads in gleaming coils. My mother's terrier removed the sweetbreads once and carried them all the way upstairs and laid them by my bed so that my bare feet sank into them first thing in the morning. Other cheerless sights included the amputated dusty stumps of twenty-four geraniums, kept in their pots forever in the hope that one day they might live again. These had been eaten by the Shetland pony I had taught to come into the house. My husband—an American—asked why I taught the Shetland pony to come into the house. Because, of course, as any reader will understand, that is what you want a pony to do, just as you want a duck to sit on your lap and watch television. Just once a year, in early winter, we were encouraged into the kitchen and lifted onto chairs to stir the Christmas Pudding, black, unctuous, bejewelled with silver threepenny bits, and a single mother-of-pearl button, the bachelor's button it was called.

Such were the offerings fed to the Aga, who sometimes looked kindly upon them, and sometimes not. Its disfavour, usually expressed in sullen sulphurous darkness, occasionally took strength from another shift of the wind; then the hot plates and the simmering plates would glow in a brilliant, translucent red and the mighty altar would shudder convulsively and the chimney would roar not only like the wind but like the ocean. Years later I read in *Wuthering Heights* of Heathcliff's eyes "like the clouded windows of Hell" and thought at once of those raging metal surfaces.

There was an interregnum of some years, when Esperanza and her sisters came from Spain and ousted the resident tyrant, to rule the kitchen. They placated the Aga and coaxed it to provide perfect paella and most exquisite meringues. The family moved freely in and out of the kitchen. Our mother sang some of the happier

Scottish hymns to herself and gave dinner parties. At night I and my older siblings sat on the Aga lids smoking cigarettes and swinging our legs in a devil-may-care manner. The Aga did not scorch us, and Esperanza did not tell on us, for she carried a deep anger in her heart that left no room for other resentments: when letters came from Spain in envelopes whose stamps bore Franco's image, she would seize the great black chopping knife and stab him again and again; then her sisters took their turn; how their eyes flashed and their bosoms heaved; how heavy the air grew, dense with imprecation and the swirl of long black plaited hair.

In my own years of motherhood, a condition from which I now wish to abdicate, I too became the custodian, or should I say guardian, of an Aga. I concluded then that the Aga of my early life had been a household god of extreme temperament; but time had passed and doubtless things had improved. Wasn't that what happened with time? I can only suppose I thought this because I was bemused by the enchanted mirage of one's children's early infancy; five of them, so various, so beautiful, so new. I made rice puddings and Stone Age loaves. I even made porridge. I thought I was an Earth Mother. The baby goat jumped on the hot plate and scorched his tiny hooves. My husband remarked that Hell would smell like this. Heedless, I brought dying kittens to life in the bottom oven, and hatched chicks. Only once did the Aga play me false. A downward swoop in temperature produced a clutch of stillborn Marans. "*Marrons glacés*," observed the family wit. The rack above the Aga dried baby clothes, then football socks, then rugby shirts and teen frills, poignantly recording the passage of time. The chief cat lay there, golden limbs extended; occasionally a paw curved down to claw the scalp of a passing punk or poet. The junior cats squabbled and copulated on the back ledge and the dogs snored against the warm façade. Guests jostled companionable hips in the traditional winter position of leaning on the Aga rail. If you do this too vigorously, you slide with surprising momentum sideways to the floor. My pig enjoyed observing this ritual, but resented the presence of men; a swift nip in the Achilles tendon ruined a relaxing moment for my son-in-law.

"It's the heart of the house, the Aga," people would say, always with that air of being the first to think up this bon mot. "It is, it really is," I would respond. Well, the heart grows older and the heart grows colder. One day I caught sight of my reflection in a friend's long mirror and upon that minute I ceased to be an Earth Mother. Away with the billows and bosoms, and on with the clinging black silk.

The Aga sensed my treachery; it sulked, it fumed. I propitiated, fed, riddled, dug its very expensive nuts out of the frozen earth floor of the midwinter coal shed, breaking all my new long lacquered temptress fingernails, and to no avail. As I crawled about, desperately riddling, in a last-ditch effort to make it hot enough to produce Christmas dinner, and the fuel remained opaquely black and not the tiniest chink of red appeared, the cover of the Scottish Church Hymnary came to my mind, with its bas-relief emblem of the Burning Bush and the inexorable legend *"Nec tamen consumebatur,"* "Nor yet was it consumed." Once you get that into your head, it doesn't go away. I became inured to festive occasions,

Christmas most especially, being marked by car journeys transporting the raw materials of dinner to friends' gas or electric ovens at tactful times of day, suited to them and not to me. More than once the turkey reached the table at 11 p.m. And the fumes grew worse. Aga engineers came and went, expressing gloom. Usually they said they'd never seen one like it. However, this was what professionals invariably said about my domestic appliances. These experts curiously all bore the names of geological features. There was Craig and Dale, there was Glen and Cliff, and there was Ridgway ("no e"). It was Glen who said, "This is a no-wake-up situation. And the dogs will go first." I hadn't really been listening to the first sentence, but the second reached me all right, and it shook me.

Has not the Aga a heart? Is it not a household god, an icon, a status symbol? Had I not heard a nine-year-old schoolboy ask another, "Do you have an Aga? Ours is the old-fashioned cream sort, they're the best." And had I not heard a lady of uncertain age, and provenance, say to an astonished country gent, "I'm more gentry than you. I have an Aga!"

No, no, no. The Aga had turned murderous. The Aga or the dogs? The Aga had to go. And why? "Well, the chimney's in the wrong place. So the wind's been blowing the rain straight down the chimney. And now it's all rotten inside and you're getting carbon monoxide." Ah, yes. It was dragged away in chains and beneath it I found a solitary wishbone and a pair of baby shoes in softest pink kid leather. I did not lament its passing, but it left a substantial gap in the kitchen. After a decent interval, my thoughts strayed towards a Rayburn. People told me they were much better than Agas because they would burn everything. The Aga professional Ridgway now revealed that he was also a Rayburn man. "They're all good. Except the Nouvelle," he told me. "Don't get a Nouvelle, whatever you do."

Within a few months, an earthenware OH pot had been hand-crafted for the chimney by loinclothed potters in the Gobi Desert and transported by dromedary, camel, and mule to wildest Norfolk. Now, at last, I could be the very proud owner of a racing-green Rayburn. My grown-up children came back from the real world and we all stood gazing at it, silent with admiration, and a sense of triumph, too. We had outwitted the Aga. Admittedly the Rayburn didn't burn everything; only oil, in fact. But it worked. Time sped by in this easeful, happy, modern way of life, involving constant warmth, co-operative cooking, no fumes, no filth, no effort.

One day as I was standing there admiring it, I noticed an embossed word flowing attractively across its front. How had I never before noticed this? How indeed? The word was terrible; the word was *Nouvelle*. And upon that moment the tryst was broken. In no time at all, I became aware of small malaises, and then the Rayburn ceased to heat the adventurous radiators, it rejected the water system; it refused even to cook. That was it. Finito. Kaput. Craig, or was it Cliff, was summoned.

"There's really nothing to be done. The chimney's in the wrong place. The wind's in the wrong place. And the relay's gone bad—I doubt they make replacements and you couldn't afford one anyway."

"What if there was a shift in the wind?" I ventured.

"There won't be," he said.

I heard my mother's voice wail down the wind and I smelt the burning of goat feet. Huge angry faces peered at me through shifting vapours, great floury arms wielded cleavers. My children appeared and receded like the unborn sons of Banquo; then came the scent of meringues and Gauloises, a vision of warmth, a home with a heart, all fading, impossible, gone now, illusions lost.

It will just have to stay there. I can't go through this again. The Nouvelle and I will grow Vieille together, equally useless. Bye-bye happiness, hallo Baby Belling.

THE DRESS

Long is the route from very rural Norfolk to the urban pastoral of Belsize Park, and longer still is the infernal transit of underground London between Liverpool Street and that promised land, involving vertiginous and hip-wrenching changes, bewilderment, and sequential folly, and a deep yearning just to turn round and go home. *Nostalgia* is the old Greek word for this powerful impulse and it may occur not only after ten years' battle on the plains of Troy but after a few hours of public transport, albeit confined to one day. The final entry to the promised land is achieved in a fearsome lift which shudders, halts, cries out, shudders again, and eventually is cranked up to the light of day. The travellers, packed in unwilling conjunction, eye one another, assessing the range of God's good will, glance at the notice which warns of overcrowding, do a head count, pray, or study the floor, invisible beneath too many feet.

But one late summer afternoon I was in this lift and an extraordinary thing happened. A stranger—but of course we were all strangers—a mythic stranger came last into the lift. She was not as others. People instinctively made way for her. She stood in a light-filled space, both stately and glamorous as only a goddess may be. Her hair was wild and black, her gaze abstracted, and her dress was green. This was the world's most perfect green, platonically perfect green, beyond viridian, emerald, or jade, intense and yet translucent, fathoms deep. And the dress itself flowed exquisitely, neither long nor short, bias cut, three-quarter-sleeved; romantic but formal, sculpted and flounced, flamboyant and entirely *comme il faut*, self-contradictory. In brief, it was the most beautiful dress in the world and I forgot the long journey and the steep walk ahead of me, and my purpose in coming at all to London in my absolute need to possess it.

Safely delivered to the upper air, I ventured to address the goddess, stating that this was a literally fabulous dress. She was pleased and so I dared to ask where she had found it. Norfolk. Unbelievable auspice. We parted, and I moved onward to my baby grandson, dreaming still of the green dress and haunted by Lorca's wonderful lines,

> *Verde, que te quiero verde . . .*
> Green, how I long for you, green,
> Green wind. Green branches.
> The ship upon the sea
> The horse on the mountain.
> With the shadow on her waist

She dreams on her balcony . . .
With eyes of cold silver.

And there is mention of the gypsy moon, *la luna gitana*.

———

Outside my daughter's house a mulberry tree's leaves fling glimpses of the bluest sky and its fruits splash in wanton scarlet across the pavement. The fierce and simple joy of primary colours compounds with the bliss of the baby's shining eyes and conspiratorial smiles. He is my favourite ballroom partner, and after quite a few circuits of Brahms's lullaby, he retires to his dreams and I to mine. Of the dress.

And there are more delights to come. I am woken in early morning by the delicate pacing of a horse beneath my window. A soldier riding down the crescent, his horse sheened in light. And then the sound of a mighty cataract, incomprehensible and overwhelming. Sixty-three horses pass by, stepping in harmony, three by three, one ridden, two bareback. I run down the stairs in my dressing gown, which looks much like an archaic summer dress; round the corner I rush, into the villagey square. It is thronged with horses and the early shopkeepers have set out buckets of water. Quite a few star-struck women in *déshabille* are milling about, some attached to small children. The soldiers, dismounted, stand modestly by their horses as they drink. In the warm sun steam rises from the shining flanks and there is a fragrance of tarry smoke, most delicate, like Lapsang souchong. Everyone wants to speak to a soldier, everyone wants to stroke a horse. Everyone is happy. The horses raise their heads and sigh; diamond drops glitter on their muzzles. We are all outside time, in perfect accord. And then the riders are up and gone, and the great waterfalling noise of hooves recedes into such stillness that we hear a cock crowing far, far away.

So, back in Norfolk, trapped again in the unremitting blankness of a wet, failed summer, I telephone the creator of the green dress and arrange that she shall make one for me. This is an *enormous thing for me to do*. I am a person devoid of disposable income and I never buy clothes. What is the point, when I'd be best in a burkha? The last time anyone made me something to wear was in my own early childhood. Nanny's customised bibs—purple ribbon binding—pinafores, and smocked dresses belong in that neverland of thumb-sucking and proper summers and paddling in rock pools and planning to be a princess. When one grew up. I realise that this is exactly what I am doing now. I, who have always reacted badly to remarks like "that's really you" in sartorial circumstance, believing that clothing's purpose is to conceal or transform the raw material into the unrecognisable, am now helplessly submerged by the pathetic fallacy that in achieving and wearing the green dress I shall become the desired one in Lorca's poem, the mythic creature up from the underworld, the princess of my infant aspiration.

The creator, whose voice is identical to the voice of someone I love, commands me to take measurements of utterly inaccessible bits of myself. Nape of neck to back of waist. Waist to lower shin or something. How? No one but I and she must know these terrible truths. The final statistics suggest that I am a hexagonal wardrobe.

In due course a huge parcel arrives by special delivery. The creator has told me that it contains not only the dress but a hat and a necklace and an insouciant wrap. I am very frightened. For days the box sits looming reproachfully across my bedroom. People ask me if I have tried it on. Yes, I say, it's perfect. I have talked too much about this and I am resolved that even if it fits not at all the die is cast. The dress and I must go forth together, specifically to an oncoming family wedding.

But what if the most beautiful dress in the world has now become the most hideous? I ponder the possibilities. Perhaps I'll never wear it again. Perhaps I will wear it for my funeral. Or for gardening. Or if it is still the most beautiful dress in the world, perhaps someone will be so beguiled by it that they will mistake me for the princess and I will be wearing it for a wedding of my own. Currently the only person who wishes to marry me is my black Labrador, who of course is almost perfect. But the vicar won't hear of it. O dress, are you me? Am I you?

So time goes by and the day of the wedding is with us. Even then I postpone my rendezvous with the dress until the last possible moment, painting and repainting my nails, according great and unaccustomed attention to mascara and poking the wand into my eyeball. Almost blindly the dress, the hat, and I are united. I glance in my darkling mirror and see nothing but a vague and tarnished spectre. I don't really want to see more. The hat is small and coquettish, echoing here and there the dress's green; it is plumed and veiled. I have never worn a veil before, but it definitely seems a good thing. On the way to the wedding through marshland

and cornfields and wet skies which will be struck by vast revolving shafts of sun as the bride enters the ancient church, my escort makes favourable comment upon the ensemble. However, as he often tells people, he is a Scottish, Irish, Roman Catholic, homosexual, orphaned, working-class poet. So what does he know?

As the service begins the veil seems a less good thing. During hymn number one, it becomes fatally entangled with my reading spectacles. I shouldn't have been wearing them anyway, as I know every item in the hymnary by heart.

My panicked daughter and I struggle tearfully and silently against the fragile but very stubborn black lace. Eventually my useless specs are disentangled, just in time for the first prayer. As I don't know the prayer, I need my specs again. Nonchalantly I cast the veil aside. I can see at last.

At this point it occurs to me that actually no one is looking at me anyhow and the wedding is for the bride and groom. They stand together in archetypal beauty beneath a window of sea water glass beyond which rears the tree of life. In that church there is always the stirring of wind, even when the surrounding cornfields stand dazed and motionless in summer heat. Once I saw a pair of pigeons hatch on a stone windowsill and stretch their skeletal wings to dry in the sighing air. It is said that Anne Boleyn's remains were taken from the Tower and buried secretly here beneath an anonymous slab, in the church built by her family. Her spirit haunts it, sometimes in the form of a hare, a witch's familiar. She too wore a green dress, celebrated by her wilful spouse in the song "Greensleeves."

Later, out in the graveyard in the windy sunlight, the bells clamour and everyone is joyful. I no longer care whether or not my dress is beautiful. I am not a dress. A dress is not me. The idea has leapt and flamed and burnt itself out. I look as from a great height at people happy among the ancient tombs. There is the bride and the tower and the whirling birds. Far over there in the shade of a yew tree someone is laughing, someone in a green dress. A ghost? Myself? It doesn't matter now.

SPRING

"And so, at last, we have come through," declared D. H. Lawrence on a fine, joyous morning of spring. "For lo, the winter is past, the rain is over and gone: the flowers appear on the earth, the time of the singing of birds is come, and the voice of the turtle is heard in our land" is Solomon's less concise, but sublime, celebration, with its extra little unplanned frisson of making quite a few people think that he is talking about tortoises coming out of hibernation. After the drab skies and unrelenting cold, how sharply the natural world impinges on our senses in April. Each morning I wake to a jubilation of geese across the river, clamorously welcoming their infants and stomping to and fro as though in jackboots. Once again the heart trembles over little lambs and all this renewal speaks treacherously of a second chance, and forgiveness of the past, which is far more beguiling than the grim and lost intentions of New Year. But it's not all bird song and lambkins. The bright air stirs ancient dust through houses, windows are dingy, insects bestir themselves, spiders leap from taps. Nettles are suddenly everywhere, and ground elder too. Ivy twines through an upstairs window and nesting birds crash down chimneys. It's a time of ambivalence, advancing and retreating. In one poem Gerard Manley Hopkins wrote ecstatically, "Nothing is so beautiful as Spring"; in another he sees its abundance as a cruel taunt: "See, banks and brakes / Now, leavèd how thick! lacèd they are again / With fretty chervil, look, and fresh wind shakes / Them; birds build—but not I build; no, but strain, / Time's eunuch, and not breed one work that wakes." So much depends on one's well-being, physical or mental.

For myself, my apprehension of the natural world has been and still is unrepentantly anthropomorphic. A post-war childhood of Beatrix Potter, *The Secret Garden*, Bambi, Arthur Rackham's glowering trees, Woodland Happy Families, the singing sands, and beasts that talk—I don't really see how it could be otherwise, although I have outgrown wanting to dress rabbits in blue shorts and pugs in tutus.

Recently I watched an old home movie. There I am, whispering complicitly into my pony's ear and careering off along the glen. She understood everything that I said, and we were more or less one creature. Oh, sorrow. The film reveals that she is bored and sullen, longing for the peace of her stable; grudgingly she transports a lopsided rag doll with flailing pigtails. But nothing can warp the memory of my jackdaw, who lived unconfined in my bedroom, free to come and go as he pleased. Outdoors I would call his name three times, and he would appear, a tiny speck in the shifting clouds, zigzagging through chasms of light and wind down to my shoulder. He tried to entice me into my pocket to build a nest, and he hopped beside me up the great staircase, when he might have flown. I was lucky to grow up in a landscape of great beauty, pine forest and moorland, which fed the imagination with wild romance. I live now in another beautiful place, marsh and river, ivy-hung oak trees, and the floating white owl who at dawn, from my chimney, shrieks defiance at all the valley's other owls as they return from hunting. Lying awake and listening to this confusion of hoots and squawks and whoops, I will switch on my lamp and be joined immediately by a dozy winter wasp who must be caught and tipped out into the cold, fatal air. This is my territory, and the wasps have their own, in the attic above. For years they have nested there and mysteriously lived on into winter. Different wasps built a nest on the tip of a beech bough, at the edge of a small wood. One day it had blown to the ground and split open. Inside the tiny creatures lay profoundly still, densely packed in their hexagonal cells, and it seemed profane to be looking at them. And then they made me think of that cult of shaven-headed, purple-shrouded people who committed mass suicide in the belief that thus they would enter eternity with the comet Hale–Bopp. What a dreadful name for a comet. One thing leads to another in the natural world and its influence on the wandering mind. Susan Sontag once defined camp as an oak tree in winter. I have thought that a cormorant, cruciform, drying its wings would do as well. You may imagine my rapture when I came upon *fifteen* cormorants perched about a dead and isolated oak tree. I have lurked there, hoping for some wing-drying, but so far it hasn't happened. Heavy horse foals on parade might also qualify, for the glorious way they raise their hooves.

Nature and mankind have contrived intriguing mysteries. The hyacinth in Greek mythology springs from the blood drops of the dying youth Hyacinthus, slain by a jealous god. It is said to bear the letters *alpha* and *iota*, commemorating his cries of agony— where are these letters? The bluebell is described as *non scriptus*— not written on, to differentiate, so someone (Linnaeus?) has taken this seriously. Also in ancient Greece, at the time of Pan's festival, people liked to thrash their statues of the god with bunches of hyacinths. Bizarre and clearly impossible. Or is the hyacinth not the hyacinth, and why not? Why is there no classical Latin word for rat? There is no rat in Virgil's list of farmyard pests in the *Georgics*, no rat in Juvenal's description of the vileness of city life. Speaking of Virgil, who liked to present himself as a countryman, son of a beekeeper, how did he get away with claiming that baby bees are found under flower petals and borne to the hive in the jaws of a heroic leader bee (over oceans if required). Why do beech woods in spring at once make one think of cathedrals—rather than the other way round? But these are questions that may remain enjoyably unanswered, just as one may take pleasure in nature's triumphs and anomalies. From the security of indoors, it is a fine thing to watch, beyond a friend's clifftop garden wall, the cagouled upper torsos of ramblers in silhouette against the evening sky; as darkness falls, at one stroke of Mother Nature's wand they are transformed into a column of rats moving one by one in stealth along the wall. Later the rats will move to the windowsill and peer in; their eyes glitter in the candlelight. The writer Colette was distressed, almost afraid, when she saw her mother exultant over a blackbird who had out-witted their scarecrow and continued to ravage their cherry tree. This lady shared her evening bowl of chocolate with a spider who would descend promptly on its thread of gossamer, reeling itself back to the ceiling when sated.

Civilisation's curious balance of retreat from and exploitation of the natural world is what makes it possible for us to indulge in such pleasures. No one would wish to experience hurricanes and typhoons directly. Contrasts are needed. The freezing beauty of a starlit night is complemented by a house that is warm. Nature is neither friendly nor hostile, but as Housman said, heartless and witless: the relationship is one-sided. Always remember that just as you can eat every bit of a pig, so it can eat every bit of you.

PORTIA

It was on Christmas morning three years ago that I first met my pig. In a shadowed corner of the barn a heap of straw shuddered, was still, shuddered again. The children stood solemn and expectant. Motes of dust floated off the straw into the cold bright day and nothing happened. Then she was there. As a submarine surfaces, so a small black snout emerged, two blunt triangular ears, a cubic little creature, Medium Vietnamese with a snippet of Berkshire. She was quite wild then, and I spent many hours in the bleak January afternoons sitting on the barn floor, talking, coaxing, offering apples while she remained as far away as possible, always in profile, wearing an expression of intense cunning. It was cold and boring and I began to brood about my middle years and how very little I wanted to spend them like this. The daughter who provided the piglet had retreated to New York and central heating and glitzy urban life. Everyone else was in London doing grown-up things. I remembered that in childhood

I could spend all day sitting about with animals, indulging in anthropomorphic fantasies. Not now, not any more. And a pig is for life, not just for Christmas. One afternoon, as I was wondering how long they live for anyway, she tiptoed towards me, seized the apple, and reversed, chomping and champing and foaming at the mouth. Her little eyes glittered with triumph. I could see that she thought that she had outwitted me. So it was that our relationship began, on the strict understanding that she was cleverer than I was, and would do things her way only.

The pig's name was Portia and she was kind enough to respond to it, trotting nimbly from the bramble thickets and sere marsh grasses which represent my garden. More spectacular results could be gained by singing her special rather simple song: "She's a pig, she's a wig, she's a piggy wig wig, she's a wiggy piggy girl." Gruesome as this sounds, it was well worth it to see a gambolling pig, a pig fleet of foot, bucking and caracoling. She was free always to wander where she pleased and she showed a strong sense of territory, only twice ever straying beyond the bounds of my domain. It was on Easter Monday that she chose to visit the village and hold up the thronging holiday traffic. Suffering from city dementia, motorists were crying: "It's a wild boar." Photographs were taken, people got out of their cars and daringly approached, but not too near. Portia was oblivious, she was licking a squashed hedgehog up off the tarmac. My sons, sallying forth to a drinking bout, were obliged to intervene; she would not move. The novelty had faded and the traffic jam wished to inch forwards. There was nothing for it but to sing her song. Alert, responsive, the pig raised her head, listened for a moment, and sped back up the drive. The boys cowered in the hedge, uncool forever.

Her other excursion did not go so well. This time she was found uprooting shrubs in Mrs. Hooker's garden. Mrs. Hooker was absent, enjoying an afternoon at the Young at Heart club, but Will, her neighbour, tried to lure Portia homewards. This didn't work. He tried to shoo her; this worked even less. A pig at bay glowered from the splintered shards of the flowering currant bush. Summoned by a child, I ran down the drive to find that Will had just lassoed her. She somersaulted, she reared, she flung herself about like a dervish. And she screamed. I had never heard such screams; Jack the Ripper might have been doing all his victims simultaneously. They could be heard four miles away at the Young at Heart club. Then came silence. Will had pulled the lasso off but the pig knew nothing of it. She had passed into a catatonic trance; she was a stone pig, standing on her four short legs, breathing lightly but completely out of it.

I was distraught. I thought she would die. She must die at home. Just as one might move a statue, so we transported her up the drive, lifting, setting down, lifting. She did not flicker an eyelash. But as we reached the house the puppy came bounding out. The puppy was fond of Portia and Portia enjoyed his company. Together they would lie on the grass and snuff the breeze. Sometimes they and the nasty dwarf pony played chasing games, taking it in turn to pursue and be pursued, always skidding to a stop before collision. Now the puppy was licking Portia's terrible staring face. And now her snout trembled, and her ears flickered, her eyes focused. Very slowly she came back to life.

Another puppy, a terrier, had a less romantic encounter with the pig one windy summer afternoon. This I observed from a distance, helpless in my car. There stood the pig, gazing dreamily up at the shifting clouds, and there, behind her, horribly attached, was the terrier, pumping vigorously. This monstrous incident did not produce any pogs or digs, and I believe that Portia was quite unaware of it, her personal geometry being such that she is unable to turn round except by executing a U-turn. Nonetheless she has been a trim and active pig, and she used to enjoy going for unambitious walks with me until some officious person pointed out the dangers and legal red tapes attached to the business of Pig Movement.

On one particular idyllic stroll through silent woodland she spotted a man in the distance and fled to the church for sanctuary. From infancy she has disliked most men, especially my son-in-law and my middle son, both of whom she has bitten. She bit them because they were in the kitchen where she liked to be. Her favourite upright position was leaning against my legs under the kitchen table. When she had done this for long enough, she would emerge and chuck a few chairs around, using her head as a battering ram and catapult. Like many pigs, she had a boisterous hooligan side to her nature, and a great relish for effect. Slamming doors was another satisfying pastime. Her extraordinarily acute sense of smell led her to go through handbags to extract an apple, to identify cartons containing fruit juice, and on one occasion to steal a rustic wine box containing some fine Bulgarian vintage. She was furtive with the wine box, scuttling up the kitchen with it clamped in her jaws. Beneath the window she paused and set it on the floor; resting one trotter firmly on top she gashed the box with a single snap of those lethal incisors. A ruby fountain sprang towards the ceiling, falling back gracefully to rise again and play about the pig. Noisily she drank, catching the liquid as it leapt, catching the joy as it flies. Through the window the sun shone from the bright blue heaven; the pig stood ankle-deep in her alcoholic lagoon and still the fountain played. Her fondness for wines does not extend to beer, a draught popular with many pigs of lesser sensibility, but on the evening when she had consumed a bowl of whisky trifle, a silent and balletic pig pranced beside me through the dusk towards the barn. Her tastes in food are demanding; not for her the bucket of pig slops, potato peel, and vegetable trimmings. Salad is acceptable only if dressed with olive oil, carrots are too dull to contemplate, and you can keep your brassicas. But ratatouille and pumpkin pie provoke cries of ecstasy which I can only liken to sex noises on television.

While she is not an asset in the garden she is not destructive; she learnt quickly that she should not lie in flowerbeds, and she does not normally go rooting. She is addicted to geraniums, one tiny vice. In hot weather she will lie in the shade or wallow in a paddling pool or dig a shallow grave to serve as a dust bath. In all these activities she reveals a nature which is profoundly sensuous, mirroring the voluptuous curves of her swaying roseate belly and belying the staccato elegance of her small black feet. Certain members of my original Scottish Presbyterian family cannot bear to look at her. Not so the local Labour candidate, however. I spied him with his red rosette coming up the garden and shrank behind the curtains. The pig lay slumbering on the lawn. The candidate peered round and, feeling unobserved, bent down and kissed the sleeping beauty. She jerked into consciousness, saw the red rosette, saw the man, and fled, doing her Jack the Ripper shrieking. Red as his rosette, the candidate knocked on the door. Neither he nor I mentioned the incident.

This hatred of men is a big nuisance when things go wrong. Portia's medical attendants have to be wooed from far-flung outlying areas where they have women vets. I had to try three different practices before I could find a vet (female) who was willing to cut her toenails—it is impossible for me to do this because she goes into Jack the Ripper mode immediately. Pigs die from stress, and they die from shock in anaesthesia. They are a nightmare to treat. I had tried unsuccessfully to obtain some anti-stress homeopathic pills to proof her against the toenail ordeal, and was startled when the homeopathic doctor advised me to have a police surgeon standing by since it seemed there might be an element of violence. After this disappointment I did find a female vet who refused to come because she had trimmed three of another man-hating pig's feet, carefully doing each foot on a different Wednesday, and after the third visit the pig had lain down and died. At last an intrepid young woman arrived, accompanied by a nurse, and sedated the pig with a blow dart in the manner of David Attenborough and the white rhino. Even this modest tranquilliser, she warned, was potentially lethal. It didn't seem to work, and a second dart was blown. The pig shrieked piteously, her whole being concentrated in one gaping set of jaws. The nurse and I cornered the pig with an old trampoline; the vet hung upside down from the barn wall, there being no space left in the improvised corner; the toenails were cut from the upside-down position; and the screaming went on. I thought I, too, might die of stress.

Indian summer brought tranquillity to the pig; she winnowed the harvest field by moonlight, stately but agile on her smart new trotters. One late autumn afternoon I walked beneath a wild cobalt sky; seagulls planed on the wind high over the sepia oak trees, and long shafts of light shed random radiance. On a distant slope a huge pig stood, invested suddenly with unearthly glory. Beyond, his fellows rootled disconsolately in the mud, consigned to outer darkness. I mused then on fate's inconsistencies and thought that despite everything mine was a lucky pig. I should not have had that thought; or perhaps it was doom's harbinger.

For now, after a life so full of peril and pleasure, the pig has turned her face to the wall. Since October she has refused to leave her barn. She is in deep melancholia and she throws her water round her stall, flinging the bowl contemptuously out the door. She eats, she sleeps, and that's it. I have tried music, companionship, cats, toys, bunches of soothing herbs, mulled wine, and Rescue Remedy. Nothing works. I don't know what to do. A wise woman called one day and she suggested that Portia might be pining for maternity. This could lead ultimately to eleven melancholy pigs facing the barn wall. I might become a latter-day Circe. These pigs could never be for eating, but pigs are not popular now as pets; indeed, I believe pig sanctuaries are opening. "Their day has gone," someone said the other day. "Like the alligators in New York." *O tempora, O mores.*

AMPHIBIANS

Ten years ago a man came and dug me a pond. The pond was tear-shaped, reflecting my lachrymose widowish ways, and when the garish orange digger raised its jaws for its final swoop, rills and trills and spills of water leapt joyously from the slick, slack mud. Within days, the pond brimmed full and trickled gently into a primrose-thronged ditch and thence into the river; days passed and miraculously it retained its level. The ancient Greeks had the beautiful notion that within the marble block the statue waits for release; so in that dull clay I like to think that until this moment the trapped spring had seethed and gurgled unbeknown, now to revel in crystalline liberation.

I had wanted a pond so that I might become acquainted with newts, and so that I might grow grey-blue irises; I would be seen by visitors, peering out at them, wearing a faded fisherman's smock and carrying a trug. The grey-blue irises have not happened, nor the smock, nor the trug. Instead nature has provided yellow flags and purple water mint. But newts arrived immediately, mysterious and magical as the spring itself.

It is important, when considering newts, to clear the mind of Ken Livingstone and pigeon culls and bendy buses. Red Ken has no place here. Newts are aquatic salamanders; they are ancient and wise and mythic; they are efts. An eft became a newt at some point in another mysterious process, linguistic this time. Other delightful creatures joined the newts. One morning in early spring I saw frogs dancing in courtship; they leapt high out of the water and dropped down in a great splash. Water voles sped across the lily pads, crossing the pond with the briefest of immersions, "just like Jesus," observed my small grandson, his eyes bulging like lollipops. Toadlets loped through the grass and the horrifying and weirdly named nymphs of dragonflies patrolled the murky floor, grimly helmeted and murderous. It is not generally known that these exquisite and ephemeral beauties spend almost all their lives as underwater exterminators in hideous disguise. My family, too, appeared in the pond. We watched the total eclipse of the sun reflected there. The garden was silent, tranced in eerie dark green light; trees were suspended upside down in the water and among them gleamed the drowned images of my sons and daughters and grandchildren. I stood on the far side and thought of the underworld.

So for years the pond's life remained apart and intact, providing intrigue and excitement and otherness. But of late I have become aware of its impinging on my existence in unthought manner. Due to a sequence of ill-executed hip operations, I have taken to sleeping downstairs. So it was that I felt a flicker of movement in my slipper, and paused; out leapt a tiny black toad. What I had thought the skeleton of a leaf on the rug by my bed turned out to be a flattened newt. In the dark shadows of the hallway, creatures scuttled and lurked and compressed themselves under furniture or crouched motionless in corners. The invasion of the amphibians had begun.

Or, perhaps, it had always been there, coming and going, unnoticed, nocturnal. For ancient memories may persist in these infinitely delicate creatures, prompting them down the pathways of their ancestors, who have passed this way, variously leaping and loping and creeping, even from a time when this part of my old house did not exist. They make their inexorable passage under doors, they thrust themselves up between flagstones, if need be they will clamber. Like the ducal trains in Shakespeare's plays, a procession of newts may move side by side with one of toads. "Did not I dance with you in Brabant, once?" enquires Berowne of Rosaline as she goes by in parallel procession. Headstrong and skittish the lass ripostes, "Did not I dance with you in Brabant, once?" Just so, I have seen a newt and a toadlet advance and retreat, swirl and sidestep, perform their sarabande along the hall. And all's well that ends well indeed, except it's *Love's Labour's Lost*.

I have observed that people are sympathetic to newts, or at least to the idea of them. They watch newt television programmes and subscribe to newt rescue funds. Toads in the house are quite another matter; they don't want to hear about them, and they don't want to see them. Few there are who are willing to pick them up and carry them out to safety, away from the crushing foot and the sadist cat. My pet pig Portia used to chase them too, but she has gone. Now I am the lucky legatee of a great quantity of gauntleted Marigold gloves, black and suggestive of fetishistic practice. Naturally I, as a Scottish gentlewoman, would never purchase such items; they are the gift of my American husband. And toads should be lifted carefully, in bare hands, which are cupped, and closed. The exudation from their nubbly skin serves as a cure for warts and verrucae, and is of course totally wasted on black Marigold gloves. Who would ever be rescued by a black Marigold? Not I. Not Fay Wray. Why then a toad? In Ireland, where toads are supposed to have been banned by St. Patrick, they are nonetheless known, along with poets, as warty boys. Once I was engaged to a poet who was walking before me up a muddy path when I saw a frog bound to confront him. "Mind the frog!" I cried. "Fuck the frog!" he responded, treading on it. That was the end of that, and I married another, and better, poet. I mention this incident only to show that I have a long rapport with amphibians who have at least in this instance shaped my life. Only thrice to my knowledge have I interfered with an amphibian's life—once the aforementioned flattened newt. And I brought back to life a tiny jewel froglet who had been paralysed by a floating and domed water spider, only to have it snatched from my fingertips and consumed by a passing hen. And once I transfixed an adult frog on the prong of a garden fork. This horrible moment was used by my heartless publishers on the cover of the paperback edition of my novel *O Caledonia*.

At this eftling time of year miniature frogs hiphop bright as dewdrops among the posies of heartsease and chamomile which adorn the stubble field. Dusk descends, then moon and stars. I sit in the darkness outside and listen to *le transatlantique* play Chopin's Barcarolle on his concert grand. A pinpoint of light gleams beside me; a newt is curved over a nasturtium leaf, its hands delicately splayed, its eyes reflecting the heavenly spheres; it is intent on its own secret life. When I go indoors it may follow, or it may not. And we may pass in the night, without signal, but on my part, with a poignant sense of privilege that our lives should ever cross.

DOG DAYS

Dogs are us in heart and soul, but better. How privileged we are to love them and know them and make guesses about them, and how painfully do we even as infants learn that the price of love is loss, but also that love and memory will outlive death. I feel that all my lifelong great loving of dogs has been threaded through with the fear of death, the unbearable knowledge that their days are so much fewer than ours. Only from earliest summers do I recall an untroubled love; the moment when the sea chills into dusk, the sands are suddenly cold, and you run from the water and fling yourself into the warm fur of the golden retriever, Rab the hero dog. His birthday was in May. Enthroned and robed in the scarlet gown of St. Andrews University, he would preside graciously over the dining table. His festive tea included birthday cake, of course, and his favourite dog pies, available to this day in superior shops, and known to the English as Scotch pies.

It was said that he had saved our father's life and also that Polish airmen had kidnapped him and he had found his way over many months all the way back to the north of Scotland from a place called Aldershot. On his birthday we children read him poems we had composed commemorating these and other exploits, some, alas, involving sheep and hens, Rhode Island Reds and white Leghorns in particular. There were dark times when he and his assistant, the junior dog, an Irish terrier, wore the cumbrous corpses of these birds slung round their necks to teach them a lesson. They did not learn their lesson, and hen-keeping was abandoned. Sheep-harrying continued, however, but somehow Rab eluded the police, the farmers, the gamekeepers and their guns. Often he was tethered on a very long and inconvenient rope which tripped everyone up at the bottom of the stairs. Or for weeks he would spend the hours of daylight brooding sombrely in his car, an abandoned 1915 Armstrong Siddeley which my brother had destroyed by reckless driving on the unmade hill roads. And, as often as not, on the twilight moment of release he would be off again, up to the moors and taking the more circumspect terrier with him. What wretched sleepless nights I endured, convinced that this time they would not return. Rab lived until he and I were both eighteen years old. More than going to university, or possessing a Hebe Sports tweed suit, or being offered a pink gin, his death marked for me the end of childhood. Eighteen years may seem a long while to be a child, but in those days there weren't teenagers and I certainly had no plans to be a grown-up. I see him now, a golden dog running through a storm of seagulls at the water's edge, under the great clouds of summer.

How kind the dogs were all those long years. When they were not intent on nocturnal blood sports they slept like tombstones on our beds, their solid presence driving the ghouls far away. They were particularly helpful with the dreadful business of mealtimes, when you were expected to chew everything thirty times and leave nothing on your plate. Luckily we always used table napkins, in which a sly disgorgement might be ferried from lip to lap and thence to the silent canine jaws waiting beneath the table. Of course if we were not being watched, a quick flick of the wrist was all that was needed. I employed this dexterous technique quite recently at a glum dinner party, where the host was drunk, the hostess was trembling, and the food was grey. Grey mushroom soup gave way to grey risotto which gave way to grey pecan pie. I could eat no more, but I had spotted a handy terrier cruising by. I thought with John Keats, "This creature hath a purpose and its eye is bright with it." Swift as lightning my pudding sped beneath the snowy reaches of the damask cloth, instantly triggering an almighty invisible dog-fight. Everyone shot under the table, where not one but two iden-tical terriers were up on their hind legs locked in mortal combat. Between them lay a great grey triangle of pie. Everyone saw this and no one knew it was mine. Indeed, there was some foolish spec-ulation about how it could possibly have got there.

Whatever sort of dog one has at any given time, that sort will always be the best; this applies to the chief dog. The junior dog may be of a different breed, which will of course be favoured, but not to a dogmatic (ha) extent. So for nearly two decades my paragon was a golden retriever. Since then there have been other wonderful dogs. When first we moved from London to the country I presented my husband with a Doberman pinscher whom he christened Matthew Arnold Revisited, Jockey of Norfolk. The rest of us called him Dobe. Dobe at once made it his business to ensure our social isolation. Adoring, docile, beloved and somnolent at home, he would sally forth from the end of our drive in an alert and independent frame of mind. Motorists would be startled and then enraged to find him slavering horribly, fangs embedded in their nearside front tyre, or pursuing them along the road barking in an excruciating high frequency. Bicyclists likewise had short shrift. Sometimes there was a tumble, sometimes there was a brief appearance before the magistrates. Villagers were not to leave their houses. If they ventured forth, just crossing the road, perhaps, to go to the shop, he would be there, rounding them up, leaping in circles and doing his crazy bark, driving them into the red telephone kiosk. There he would stalk back and forth on his hind legs, pressing his muzzle against the glass panes, dribbling and munching suggestively, while his prisoners, incoherent with fury, dialled our number to demand release, and repayment for the call, and punitive redress. He used to escort my minivan, attached to the wheel and barking, the four miles to the children's tiny primary school; there he would gallop joyously about the playground, indiscriminately licking little faces. "Call him by his name, dear," cried Miss Clark. Some hope. The whole tyre-chewing, slavering, barking business would be repeated as I drove home. He knew how to open doors and windows and so could let himself in and out of the house as he pleased. His greatest ambition was to bring down a plane. To this end he raced about the prairie field, his hind quarters displaying the rotary action so admired by connoisseurs of the breed. He hurled himself intermittently into the air, pawing at the sky. Fast living overtook him in the end. He returned one morning from seeing off a Fairchild A10, a low-flying warplane, flung the back door open, surged into the kitchen, and dropped dead. It was very quiet after he had gone and I had to admit that it was nice to go to the village without his overweening company. I even painted his favourite room pink and hung up floral curtains, impossible hitherto because of his window-opening. Then I felt guilty and took them down. The pink walls soon faded back to wood smoke and nicotine brown.

Oh, what a gallimaufry of dogs memory brings, each one so loved and special. The deerhound steps his airy way towards me, his head tilted in gentle self-deprecation. He was bred by the late and great Anastasia Noble of Ardkinglas, whom I last saw in her quiet splendour at a gathering of deerhounds in the fens. The purpose of the meeting was said to be hare coursing, but the hares kept low in the dykes and the deerhounds, losing sight of them, so lost interest, and took to racing and leaping and caracoling. The spectral dogs, the freezing December skies, and the vast empty landscape hang motionless before me, gathered all beneath Miss Noble's ghostly benediction. That is one aspect of heaven, in winter. A springtime glimpse reveals a haze of bluebells, shadowed by beech trees just coming into leaf. Two figures on grey horses pass among the silvery trunks; one of them might be me. Beyond, in a sunlit glade, the deerhound dances. There can be no heaven without dogs. I know this for a fact; our old vicar told me. In his seven churches dogs were always welcome.

Thinking of deerhounds makes me think of lurchers, dogs I may no longer keep due to problems with a nearby commercial enterprise involving pheasants. As one might put it. Graceful and loyal, lurchers are the most inward of dogs, in habit peripheral, delicate and fleeting as shadows. A brindled lurcher will fade into an old chintz sofa, or a gravel path, or dappled shade in the flicker of an eyelid; or again will dissolve into those great shafts of sunlight which move across the stubble in late summer. Lurchers are the most accomplished and elegant of all thieves; they run exquisitely through streams, their slender legs shimmering, beaded in silver droplets. They are swift, silent killers and unbelievably accident-prone. They cost a bomb in vet's bills and they are worth every penny.

But now I can't have lurchers, not even on a visit, and I have wandered, by the chances that beset the dog lover, into the enchanted realms of the Labrador. Are Labradors not divine? The very word, delightful to enunciate, demands a capital letter. One of the Mitford sisters, employed in Spain during the Civil War as some sort of booking clerk, was relieved to find great numbers of Labradors leaving their warring land and always made sure they had the best travel accommodation possible. Eventually of course she was disillusioned; they were not dogs, but *labradores* (workers). Still, as a communist she could hold on to their preferential treatment. Our Labrador line began with Honey, given to us by a game-keeper because she was gun-shy. She changed her mind about this, and at the sound of shooting would slip off and join the fray with such tact and efficiency that people kept trying to buy her, and once someone stole her. She had a lifelong and fully requited illicit love affair with the farm collie down the road, producing one hundred and twelve puppies of great charm and distinction. We kept one of them, a delightful but caddish black-and-white hound. When Honey died he sat with proper solemnity by her grave, but as she was lowered in he realised it was lunchtime and left, returning in a few minutes to resume his vigil. He had cleared the kitchen table, but this was his last act of caddery, for now he was the senior dog, with family responsibilities. I am inclined to think that the early caddishness came from his collie side; in latter life he was the very soul of warmth and loving kindness, every inch a Labrador. Then there came Dido, rescued from a broken home, the fattest Labrador ever seen. "With the owner's co-operation," intoned the vet into his special recording machine for matters of importance, "Dido has now lost twenty-six kilograms." She took to digging up radishes to cheer her tiny meals. A black Labrador puppy joined us. My son named him Hannibal after the Carthaginian general, not the serial killer, though now I think of it, the general was even more of a serial killer. Hannibal and Dido ran away into the woods. I stood wailing, "Hannibal, Dido," over and over into the autumn wind and was surprised to hear another voice issuing from the beech trees.

"Cassiopeia, Cassiopeia," it cried. We joined forces, agreeing that we were very stupid embarrassing people to give our dogs these silly names. Joggers were sneering at us. Joggers. Cassiopeia proved to be a flat-coated retriever. On a similar occasion I encountered a woman shrieking for Horace; we discussed this name business while the dogs didn't come back, and she said she'd named him after the great Roman poet. "I loved Latin at school," she said. "No one else did, except for one other girl. But she was very peculiar and chewed her pigtails and wouldn't speak." In no time we discovered that we had been at school together, so long ago, in far-off Scotland, and yes, I was that silent pigtail chewer. The dogs returned, she went back to London, and we lost touch all over again. This I find is the way of coincidences. Nothing happens, they might as well not have been. Except that they were. Hannibal, for example, while browsing the grasses at the edge of the drive, makes a peculiar clonking sound with his jaws. My deceased husband used to make an identical sound eating an apple. I have never heard this noise otherwise. I had a moment of wild surmise; was it possible that George had returned to me in the form of a great black dog? But no, this was rapidly quashed. George would not have made a good Labrador. And goodness is what Hannibal is about, and wit and charm and resource and the genial engendering of unplanned litters on black Labrador bitches (only). He happens to have an astonishing pedigree so nobody minds too much. "You've got a royal dog there," said one doughty owner, instinctively removing his cap. Well, just a touch perhaps, but lots of other bloodlines too. Indeed, Hannibal's state is kingly, and I could write a great deal about him, but I should keep it for another time. He is old now and stiff and can no longer climb onto my bed; he sleeps instead on a small sofa by the window. When I wake I watch him lying there, one ear draped most delicately over the sofa back; he breathes so lightly that I think he has gone, I almost hope it, rather than find myself once again colluding with the vet in that final act of treachery which is of course all for the best. Meanwhile my husband, who seems jealous of Hannibal, has ghosted the junior dog Bluebell's autobiography, in a fabulous literary *jeu d'esprit*.

So September wanes and the early evenings are elegiac, still and scented with phlox and the straight plume of smoke going up from the bonfire. The dark shadow is there. I do not think Hannibal will see another summer. But now he is rolling on the mown grass, joyous as ever, joyous as a pup, and the sound of the piano floats from the open window. He walks towards me down the green slope with the low sun behind him; he is limned in golden light and his eyes are shining. He is a paradisaical Labrador. I would not myself mind dying if I was certain we might meet like this, in a place where Labradors swim with seals and angels.

AUF WIEDERSEHEN, PETS

In the years of maturity, poised like parasitic mistletoe midway between earth and heaven, one may find that certain long-held assumptions have become invalid; one may indeed find everything is pretty questionable, and most of all oneself. In the years of immaturity one was busy creating a persona with which to deceive everyone else. Later, in the years of motherhood, one had forgotten one ever had a self.

Now, saith received wisdom, is the time for a thorough investigation. Many secrets lie beneath the sands, so go and dig them up. Know yourself, be true to yourself, be *comfortable* with yourself.

Some people in America undergo marriage ceremonies to themselves, as seen on television. Mr. and Mrs. Me. How lovely. Personally, the last thing I want to be is myself. It is bad enough looking in the mirror. Say no more, leave the secrets in the sand, look away and forget the sad psyche. Thus the odd little self-related aperçu will come as a fresh surprise, or of course a nasty shock, but salutary in its sudden revelation, a tiny apocalypse.

One evening not so long ago I was selflessly unpinning sheets from the line in archaic rustic manner. The customary Force 8 East Anglian gale was blasting away and the sheets engulfed me, wrapping themselves round my head and shoulders, billowing and somersaulting.

So it was that I failed to notice a sly skateboard lurking beneath the washing line, so it was that I stepped on it. Joyously it sped off, bearing my mummified form into a headlong hurtle on the concrete yard. Speechless, bombinating agony, then a feeble little flicker of a thought. At least no one could see me.

Wrong as usual. On my left there was a gurgling, gargling noise and a tugging movement; on my right a high-pitched silvery screaming. There stood my pig and there stood my terrier, both staring hard at me, not with concern or sympathy, but with beady-eyed cupidity. I knew then that if I had been killed they would have eaten me. The pig had recently sampled the delights of human flesh with a mouthful of my son-in-law; she was ready for more.

That unhappy incident has affected me physically and mentally. I have an arm that aches like hell whenever I am bored, most poignantly when people are going on about income tax, the benefits of the computer, or their cat.

And I have found myself brooding over Piero di Cosimo's wonderful painting *The Death of Procris*. Procris, who has not bothered too much about getting dressed, occupies the foreground, lying in much the same position as myself, post-skateboard. She is a woman with a chequered past, but she has always meant well and does not deserve her cruel fate. However, she has done some dim things, like giving her unfaithful husband her very own unerring spear. So in the end, in the painting, there she lies, pierced by that same spear, expiring among the small bright flowers of mythic spring.

At her head crouches Pan, attentive and priapic; at her feet is her hunting dog, Lailaps. Beyond, the shore swerves and, on the strand, hounds hold a boar at bay. It is an estuary scene and a dwindling rivulet wanders its way towards the sea.

Down by the water the hounds are half-hearted, one sitting down, one approaching the boar shyly, tail half-drooping, ears flopped. A number of large birds are paying absolutely no attention. Distant headlands merge into haze and the blank indifferent sky.

The ancient Greeks had a notion that the image lay waiting to be discovered and released. So it seems to me that images deliberately lurk about in the effluvium of our lives until such time as we recognise them. They have always been there waiting for this moment.

I have loved this painting for more than thirty years, but it is only now that suddenly it speaks to me of an end to supernatural leanings, a farewell to the sympathetic fallacy. Pan's tenderness is fleeting; he has his purposes. The dog Lailaps is profoundly courteous but he is just waiting for it all to be over and then he will be down on the shore with the others. Lailaps has his own doom to fulfil; he must always catch his prey.

Looking at those figures, I realise that I have outgrown half a century's misguided involvement with animals, an exhausting series of pulsating one-sided relationships. I wish them well, but they will no longer dominate my life. When the cats go they will not be replaced. Well, I might have one but I certainly won't have six again. And a kindly detachment will be the order of the day. Ha!

What I am having, contrary to all my expectations and prejudices, is computer classes. If I try very hard my daughter may, just may, give me her discarded Mac. Then, instead of droning on about cats and dogs and pigs, I can join the queue for the e-mail monologue.

MOVING ON

It was in the brilliant light of the Antipodes that I saw myself plain. And *plain* is the word; a number of others slither to mind; middle-aged is their sum total. There I was, strolling along, not exactly singing a song, but merry and bright. And there I was, reflected in that awful full-length mirror, a shambling, shapeless she-bear, with tired eyes and a drooping mouth.

Hide, I thought, hide from the gaze of the world; and don't come out again until you're several inches thinner and fifteen years younger. If you never try on new clothes, if you believe the camera always lies, if you shrink from long mirrors as a vampire recoils from the cross, you can pretend you're getting away with the flying years.

The soft focus of presbyopia helps as well. Presbyopia was the harbinger of this new era. At first, one has difficulty reading in bed. After months of holding the book further and further away, arms extended into the freezing penumbra of a bedroom without central heating, concessions must be made.

I have a friend who snipped the sleeves off old jerseys to make arm comforters, but he, too, came to the day of reckoning, the day of the cheap magnifying spectacles available from the choicest newsagents.

"Only for reading," the new wearer proclaims. Soon they are also for chopping vegetables and then for eating anything that requires a delicate approach. Because I lose my spectacles every thirty-five minutes, I am obliged to wear them slung round my neck on a black string. They swing out and smash my grandchildren's tiny noses as I stoop to struggle with zips and shoelaces. And if I am too vain to wear them during dinner, I may be punished later by an eyeful of risotto, slyly captured on the lenses' pendant plateau.

Last summer I was in France with a friend who also required spectacles. Only for reading. Neither of us had yet evolved into string-wearing. This meant we had to stop every twenty minutes for her, every thirty-five for me, to check we hadn't lost them. I was managing rather well, better, dare I say, than she, until I found myself, speechless and sightless, confronting a menu.

My son read it out to me in rural high-school French, while my bespectacled friend mused in silence. I noticed she was wearing my specs. Mine. "So sorry, darling, they looked just like mine." Anyone could see they didn't, if they could see at all. We found hers under a bar stool at the hotel.

Thus have I learned that strings are good, vital even. They also stop you propping your specs on funny places, like your chin. And you can still see far away, into a great distance.

"We look before and after, and pine for what is not," said Shelley. Satan, too, offers this vista of temptation to anyone in middle years, a little surprised to find themselves in Dante's dark wood or, as in my case, in the dazzling sea light of the Pacific. I speak as I find. To look before and after is a sort of tautology. Which is which? Are they the same? A completing circle bringing you back to square one? I will try to look backwards, maybe before.

Well, I certainly know that I wouldn't want to go through childhood again. The anxieties, the nightmares, the foreverness of school, the longing to be a grown-up, for they were always so nice to each other. And then the big jumps, university, boyfriends, utter disillusionment. In darkness lost.

Then I had happier times, babies, five of them, spaced in a desired but unplanned manner over ten years. Now I am privileged to have grandchildren and to repeat some of those entrancements. It seems so short a time ago that their mother played in the barn, swung off that tree branch, lovingly attended by an evil little swish-tailed Shetland just as they do now.

At other times I think that I have lived as long as anyone could. My infancy is so far away, across a wide pale strand and at the end of the shore is darkness, a cave, origin. "Look homeward, Angel, now, and melt with ruth." But no malingering.

Ahead, the great doom's image lifts slowly over the horizon. Friends die, mortality moves into the immediate. I am shocked and astonished as never before by the great numbers of people in the world each, like oneself, leading their one and only precious life. I am aware, with a certain fatality, of the beats and the missed beats of my heart.

What the hell, Mehitabel? What of now? Now is as good and as ghastly as ever. I, who have skulked on the peripheries and used most tricks to get out of the serious business of living, am startled to find myself embarked on a strenuous new life with new sets of obligations. My children are grown up, and still my favourite people. They are also as alarming and nerve-racking as when they were small. My husband is dead. "You're on your own now, baby," he informed me more than once and gleefully from his hospital bed.

I miss the discipline they all imposed on my days and I find it hard to structure life around myself, despite the necessary impositions of work. This perhaps will come with practice. But from this new freedom I have learned a great deal about what I do and don't need; I have also learned to be careful about wishes, for they often come true.

And I realise now that this is a fine time. I don't care about being young or old or whatever. I am past the anxieties of earlier days, no longer concerned about image or identity or A-levels, no longer fearful of shop assistants or doctors' receptionists. I can admit, without giving a damn, to being a slut, liking salad cream, holding certain politically incorrect views. I can still change and grow, mentally and physically.

At this interesting point in life, one may be whoever and whatever age one chooses. One may drink all night, smash bones in hunting accidents, travel the spinning globe. One may teach one's grandchildren rude rhymes and Greek myths. One may also move very slowly round the garden in a shapeless coat, planting drifts of narcissus bulbs for latter springs.

MISCELLANY

THREE NORFOLK ARTISTS

Introduction to an exhibition at King's Lynn Arts Centre

I know very little about painting and drawing and I don't know what I like, so it was with great trepidation that I set off on this project. On all occasions I revealed my lack of credentials, a declared ignoramus. (Curious that there is no female form of this word. Makes one wonder, if one has the time.)

Derrick Greaves was my first port of call. He lives inland; in an old schoolhouse flooded with sunlight. It is marooned in a long green garden where purple-ribbed cabbages droop languorous leaves like elephants' ears. In the trance of afternoon dewdrops still linger on them. I tried to think of a word for their colour. *Nacreous* materialised, silent and stealthy, in the dim recesses of my skull. I kept quiet about this and asked Derrick how he would describe them. A moment's pause. "Nacreous," he said. Indoors the house feels like a ship, shining white and orderly: the steep angles of roof timbers suggest rigging and mast. Maritime, a stranded ship beneath a tree. And it is the sea which draws these very disparate artists together. I had expected talk of the great skies of East Anglia, the lure or grand illusion for so many generations of painters, but not one of them mentioned the sky; they all spoke of the sea. Furthermore each had come more or less randomly to Norfolk and found himself settling here with surprise, then slowly gathering delight. In Derrick's studio sea images proliferate. Pebbles and flints lock in a solemn watery embrace: the tattered outlines of *North Sea*, thunderous black and mauve criss-crossed by iridescence, heave like the perilous waters or form storm clouds, anchored by the steady clear line of the horizon. Conversely *Beach Fragments* is all childhood, a memory of sandy caves and starfish, beachball and shells, the curve of a leg flipping through the waves, a flounder which might be a whale or a whale which might be a flounder; you never know what will turn up at the seaside. Other drawings are dreamily erotic; lyres, flowers, corollae sway and drift in a haze of aquamarine; budding tendrils stretch hungrily towards each other. A musing on present happiness and a memory of the amniotic waters whence we came?

Angela Carter, in one of her last essays, asks, "Where was I before I was born?" She goes on to speculate that this is the primal question of life. The sea conjures such thoughts, and thoughts of death too, "So do our minutes hasten to their end." Derrick Greaves spent childhood holidays on beaches in the west of England and remembers with nostalgic warmth. Now he takes pleasure in the desolation of the winter shore, the giving and taking and treachery of the tides as they wash in broken ships and human detritus, but also scour and bleach before withdrawing. He told me with delight of his little son's comment when first he saw the sea, "It's clean." *Clean* seems to me a good word for Derrick's work. "Every inch is considered," says Anthony Benjamin. Yet there is no fuss, no clutter, instead a bold clarity which perhaps mirrors his life. "I've decided to finish with having problems," he announces. But this enviable state has not been achieved lightly and the apparent simplicity of the drawings likewise masks complexity of image and of intention. He challenges himself to "pull it off"; as he challenges viewers to unravel their own interpretations. He does not believe that this should be easy; although he describes his work as figurative, it has passed through a crucible, a melting process which removes it from representation and transforms it into art. Without pretension, and with wit.

Wit is something else all these artists have in common, wit and forbearance and generosity. I was late when I went to see Derrick Greaves, even later for Roger Ackling, latest of all for Anthony Benjamin, having lost my way yet again in an ever-increasing derangement. Feeling hotter and older and fatter every minute, I drive in circles, cursing the Highways Authority, who have so much money that they are re-laying almost every road in north Norfolk but cease to signpost villages from three miles off. On each occasion I was received with courtesy and warmth and quantities of wine. Roger Ackling lives immediately above the sea, in a clifftop coastguard's cottage. That summer day the landscape shimmered in primary colours, crayon-blue sea, golden sand, scarlet poppies in the green green grass, the sky a shade paler than the sea, idle winds softly murmuring. A bit different in winter. Roger made some inscrutable remarks about his work, chortling gently: "It's something to do with something, unless one's a liar." "If you put a stick through a spider's web what do you catch?" "I've always wanted to be a bald-headed Buddhist bowman." I was becoming apprehensive. He added that some found his stuff utterly impenetrable, while others told him that it wasn't very demanding. This always pleased him. For himself he found it best not to think. "Maybe I'm a hippy, maybe I'm a bullshitter." In fact of course he is neither, but he enjoys these peripheral skirmishes. At the cottage he leads a life of extreme simplicity, without electricity or material concerns. He gathers pieces of driftwood and crouched on the shore he burns tight gridworks of lines on to them, slanting the sun's rays through a magnifying glass. As the wind shifts there are infinitesimal variations in the patterns. He occasionally uses card instead of wood. The end result is extraordinarily beautiful, strange silver or golden tablets which appear to bear the dark and enigmatic script of some ancient, vanished civilisation, voices long silenced pleading to be heard. He describes the dots with which he composes his grid lines as "overexposed and merging photo images of the sun." Looking closely at them it is easy to capture the excitement generated by the wind's breath. If you stare long enough you can become mesmerised, so that when you look away the image seems still stamped on your retina. He claims that they are not representational, not dramatic, purely geometric. However I have always had rather big problems with abstraction and the mathematical, and I had no difficulty in transposing Roger's work into the figurative, ranging from the pre-Mesopotamian tablets to a homely Tiger Tim jersey. The great horizon which he overlooks is echoed in these tiny horizontals, the smaller the better as far as their creator is concerned. It is said that he can transport an entire exhibition in his pockets. His desire is to bring out "the smallest instance of something." Down on the storm beach, under the wind, he has the sense of being alone on the surface of the earth, a flicker in the gaze of eternity, an atom of dust dancing in the winds before the eye of Buddha. Earth, air, fire, and water; an elemental economy.

As I was leaving, an elderly gentleman appeared at the garden gate. He had made his way painfully down the long, uneven track to arrange a game of bowls with Roger, "Friday, then," they agreed. He stumbled off, back up the track. The wind was rising and little puffs of sand bombasted him. For the last five years, said Roger, this laborious assignation had been made twice a week. "But it's never happened. It never will."

Inland I drove through the poppies, in search of Anthony Benjamin, who had in fact been kind enough to send me a detailed map of his whereabouts. His studio is in a green Wordsworthian dell, within sound but not sight of the sea, and only four minutes by car from Roger Ackling. But I was coming from a different direction, and it was an hour later, after many a three-point turn in uncharted hinterlands and an unpleasant encounter with a youth who was eking out his disaffected day by lopping branches from a blooming *Buddleia* bedecked with butterflies, that I found Anthony's solitary working abode. It is a large barn, whose interior, as in Derrick Greaves's house, is white, orderly, and filled with light. I never cease to be astounded by the meticulous neatness of those who paint and draw. I can see how necessary this is, but how do they do it? All the writers I know live in a hideous shifting necropolis of skyscraper piles of books and papers regularly toppled by cats. They can never find anything, not even their special pen that Eliot once borrowed, or Ginsberg scratched his head with.

Anthony Benjamin clearly possesses the secret of eternal youth. Although he was born in 1931 he looks about thirty-eight years old. There is no point in asking him about this because it wouldn't interest him and he is reserved about the past; he asked me not to write about such parts of it as he was prepared to disclose. Suffice it to say that his battered but youthful exterior is a testament to his spirit's survival against great odds, and not to self-preservation. He has lived through turbulence and travelled far, in every sense. Now, he says, he is imposing some order on that past. He has painted, sculpted, drawn, with and without colour. At present he is working mostly in tones of grey, but colour is reappearing. His studio is impersonal, a cool, efficient working area. The light comes from glazed sections of the roof; his door is closed and he has no windows; he cannot see out. This is deliberate. He sees his work as an ongoing process, delving through genes and memory into his own expended life. His present life exists outside the studio door, separate and fresh as the trees he cannot see until he crosses the threshold. His verbal reticence is transmuted into images, abstract or figurative. "Art is always autobiographical," he says, "but also hidden, indirect." Like Roger

Ackling and Derrick Greaves he has no patience with the instant image, implicit with its packaged history, which is the currency now of much of Europe, retailed obviously by advertising and television but also in Britain by the demise of education, by Thatcherism and the cult of art as investment. Time spent in Cornwall years ago gave him a lasting appetite for landscape, now refined into landscape deployed as a philosophical outlook. I think this may be what poets do with landscape and I was not surprised to discover, at the end of the afternoon, that Anthony Benjamin reads a great deal of poetry. Both Derrick and Roger seemed to have reached a point of some peace in their lives, however transitory. I felt that Anthony had a quantity of unresolved energy and anger in him, miles to go before he sleeps. But Norfolk has perhaps offered him a respite. He watches minute by minute the changing seasons, and again the sea, surging in, brings its strange appeasement, fragments of other lives, seaweed, fossils, the enormous past. He says he will make maps of this, but not representations. I saw some reproductions of his soft grey drawings and I loved the vase of irises beside a skull. The skull is pursued by a whooshing nimbus of arcs, as though some malevolent god has just flung it down. One of the irises drops into darkness, into destruction. The others stand delicate, some scarcely delineated in their gentle glass, aloof; soon they will die. Sharp light illuminates the surface on which the vase stands perilously near the edge. Beneath is darkness, a tomb, a repository. The skull glares unforgiving from one eye socket, helpless; hopeless. Anthony showed me a poem by Wallace Stevens:

The exceeding brightness of this early sun
Makes me conceive how dark I have become.

And reillumines things that used to turn
To gold in broadest blue, and be a part

Of a turning spirit in an earlier self.

I think that's it, really. And the season changes.

So here they are, the three of them, proud, difficult, all men of integrity, a quality not much visible these days. And I do mean visible, for the work reflects the life. By their works shall ye know them. A farewell for each of them: for Derrick, a childhood memory of his own; a lonely estuary, the sands shining in early evening. And then the tide is there, the castle collapsed, gone, and the dragon flag of Wales floating out to sea. For Roger I leave an old-fashioned wooden boule so that he may adorn the turning world with air and fire. And for Anthony the Ode of Horace which begins *"Diffugere nives"* and is also wonderfully translated by A. E. Housman. Nothing should ever be easy.

THE DANCE

Jennifer was a mordant child. Her first memories were of biting and gnawing. Her teeth came unexpectedly early, "before even the first snowdrops," said her mother, who was romantically inclined but passed her days fashioning loaves in the form of lobsters, crabs, and indeterminate sea creatures armoured with crisp antennae. The broken antennae were kept for Jennifer and these were the secret of her precocious mandibles.

They lived above the bread shop; the house was thin and old and the windows looked out on the heaving grey North Sea. On winter afternoons, when sky and sea merged and the rain beat down on Cromer, her mother would draw the curtains and shiver. Then she would talk of another sea, peacock blue and peacock green, lapping white sands. A castle overlooked that sea, a castle alone on its promontory; no town, no bread shop. There she had lived, there still her mother lived. One day she would go there with

Jennifer. "You will see the sun as you have never seen it," she said in her oddly formal English.

Once on the promenade, staring at the whitening sea, she wept, but went on staring at it. The rain slashed down and mixed with her tears. Jennifer began to cry too. "In my beginning is my end," said her mother. Jennifer pulled her sleeve with numb starfish fingers and they trudged up the cliff path. The house seemed warm to Jennifer, then, and welcoming, with the scent of the bread which was always baking, or steaming and brown on racks, and her father in his white overall waving through the misted pane in the kitchen door. But her mother would pull her coat collar up as if she were even colder now she was indoors, and she ducked her head down and ran up the stairs with her nose wrinkled. There was no escape from the doughy fragrance. On the sitting room table, heaped on her mother's great Portuguese platter, azure and white as her far seas, were the day's failures or unsuccesses. "There is no such thing as failure. There is only unsuccess," said her father. Jennifer found this statement meaningless, but could see that it annoyed her mother. Anyhow, there they were for her teatime delectation, broken bread lobster pincers, and crab claws, antennae, and small warped crustaceans, and for her this was home, the smell of the bread and the crunch of the crust, the coal fire sizzling as the rain spat down the chimney, the curtains drawn and outside the great roaring sea and the lowering sky. And her mother was happy when she could not see the sea.

Later in life she could remember no summer on that northern coast, but summer must have come and gone, five times in fact, when her mother took her to Portugal. They had to fly there and then travel a whole day in a bus. Jennifer was sick a number of times, but because of her mother's excitement she was able to rise above her lurching entrails and the awful quivering, quenching heat. "Rise above it." She had heard her father shout this at her mother when she herself was tucked up in bed, had been asleep even in the warm alcove by the chimney breast above the oven. In the darkness she imagined her mother floating and lost as a seagull over the icy whelm of ocean and she clenched her fists tight and prayed for her, as if she were one of the lifeboatmen or fishermen, who went in peril on the sea.

Now the bus was bumping off the white dusty track into a village square; her mother had seized both her limp hands and was squeezing them and staring into her face with wild shining eyes. "I am happy. I am so happy," she whispered. They hugged each other. Jennifer was glad for her, but most of all she was glad to clamber off the bus and stand unsteadily in the shade, while a great shrieking gaggle of women in black flapping clothes embraced her mother and wept and embraced her again. Then they were swooping down on Jennifer. "Ah, the little beautiful." "Ah, it is at last Ginevra." The tree's low branches trembled and its leaves which were like hands waved and fanned the hot air. Fat little purple fruits plopped through them and burst in carnal crimson against the ground. The aunts trampled over them. Seeds spurted and stuck to their heavy black shoes.

The castle stood on a headland up a long hill from the village; you could not see it until you were almost there. Parts of it resem-

bled the massive fortresses Jennifer had seen in picture books; elsewhere it was dazzling white, like some of the houses in the village.
There were arcades and galleries, courtyards and fountains. Most
of the fountains didn't work. Lizards basked in the stone basins
and thin cats pounced and played among the fallen leaves which
choked them. Jennifer lay in a canopied swing in her grandmother's
special courtyard, high above a little bay and the sea, which was so
bright she could not look straight at it. Here water played gently
from an upturned urn on to a splashing cherub and behind her
she could hear women's voices, a continuing murmurousness from
upstairs windows, half shuttered now against the morning light.
That was what they did all day, her mother, her grandmother, her
aunts. They talked and they sipped iced tea and they laughed in
that shadowed room as they sat over their embroidery. Aunt Rosa
was going to have a baby, perhaps tomorrow, perhaps this very
day, who knew? Each evening Uncle Adriano came back from his
work in his pale, crumpled suit, looking excited, and they would
all smile and shake their heads. Her grandmother said, "A baby
chooses his own time. Is that not so, Ginevra?"

Jennifer had no idea how babies made their plans, but she nodded fervently, for her grandmother was the wise person, the queen
of the castle; even though she was smaller than any of them and
wore very plain clothes. There were a number of other older people
about, mostly her grandmother's sisters or sisters-in-law. They were
all widows and they looked frightening when they sat out together
on the courtyard terrace, a flock of birds of anguish, although they
smiled at her and stroked her hair as she sidled past. The only young

aunt was Aunt Jezebel, who was eighteen. Her name wasn't really Jezebel but this was how it sounded to Jennifer. Jezebel spent all day with the other women in the cool upstairs chambers or on the terrace, but she was not paying attention to them. Her round dreamy eyes stared out over the ramparts, her heavy brows contracted and her mouth turned down. She did not want to be there; not one bit. She shredded eucalyptus leaves and ground them under her heel; she moved about in an aura of camphor. This gave Jennifer a pang of wintry longing, for it reminded her of having colds in Cromer. She thought she liked Portugal, but it was very bright and it wasn't home. Soon her father was coming, and she looked forward to that, although she had the feeling that her mother did not. She had heard her mother referring to Cromer as Cromer-sur-Mer and there was something not quite right about this.

Jezebel took Jennifer to the village to meet her father off the bus. They rode down the hill on Jezebel's bicycle, with Jennifer sitting in a pannier on the back. Jezebel was happy; she sang loud melancholy songs as they went, trailing her foot round the bends instead of braking, so that the dust blew up into their faces. In the square she left Jennifer at a table under the fig trees and disappeared into the bar. By the time the bus at last came throbbing in, Jennifer was feeling very hot and very embarrassed. She did not like to sit all alone as though she were a friendless orphan; people stared at her and some children came up and spoke to her but she could not answer them and after a little they ran off, looking back at her and giggling. She chewed at her fingers and she bit her nails and she studied the ground beneath the table.

Suddenly Jezebel was leaning over her, lifting her up, pretending to be a loving aunt, and there was her father and there was a woman walking beside her father; he did not look well. His eyes glittered but his face was white. The woman was jauntily swinging a bottle by its neck. When she saw Jennifer looking at it, she stuffed it into her handbag. Her cheeks were puffy and pallid like fermenting dough; her bobbed blond hair was streaked with damp. There were subdued hugs and handshakes. Jennifer's father said the woman's name was Amicia; they were fellow travellers. He laughed after he said this, but no one else did. Jezebel had stopped looking happy and was glaring at Amicia. "Well, I guess I'll love you and leave you," she announced. "See you later, alligators," she added over her shoulder. They watched in silence as her high heels wobbled across the square to the pale green portico of the little hotel. A group of men had emerged from the bar and were watching her too. A cat with a lizard protruding from its jaws slunk round the wall of the well, snarling to itself. It looked as if it were smoking a cigar. Jennifer longed to be back in Cromer.

At lunch, in the shuttered upper room, her longing increased. Her father had been odd and quiet in the taxi from the village. "Not feeling too good; it's the heat," he said, sighing and mopping his forehead. He had to borrow clothes from Adriano; his own were far too heavy. There wasn't much conversation. Usually the women spoke simultaneously and incessantly, sometimes in English, more often in Portuguese, even at times in French, for one of the great-aunts came from Normandy. Although her mother had seemed pleased when he arrived, now, sitting next to him at the long table, she turned the other way, towards her own mother, and engaged in a discussion of embroidery silks suitable for the dress she was making for Rosa's baby. Nor was her father enjoying his plate of salt cod. He was pushing it around, nonplussed, trying to hide the glimmering and rigid fish tails under his potatoes. From her high alcove above, the Virgin Mary eyed him with displeasure.

Things seemed better the next day. Colour returned to her father's face and although the sun shone bright as ever a breeze diffused the heat. In the evening there was a party in the village square. The tables were laid out in the open and everyone danced, even the old people. In one corner bumper cars were flashing and colliding, and merry-go-round horses rose and sank and rose. The air boomed with different kinds of music and was hazy with smoke from the spits of tragic roasting piglets. Candles and bottles shone on the white tablecloths. Amicia appeared, weaving through the dancers, and joined them. She wore scarlet lipstick and she had an orange flower in her hair. She was drinking out of her own bottle, not very carefully. Pungent amber drops trickled down her chin and onto her throat. She flicked them away with a faintly grubby hand, shook her blond hair about, and pulled off her jacket. The ancient aunts sighed and looked away from her. They had smiled at her and inclined their heads. They would not do this again. At the far end of the table Grandmama's face was expressionless. Only Jezebel stared unwinkingly at those twin rotundities which heaved and quivered beyond the merest strand of black-and-yellow-dotted nylon. Only Jezebel and the men. The men who came swarming, touching Amicia's bare arm, entreating her to dance, pulling at her hands. They surrounded her, black as flies in their shiny suits. As Jennifer and her family left the square they could see her spinning about, still clutching her bottle, while the men formed a circle round her, clapping slowly, a measured clap like the beat of a funeral drum.

The old aunts went home then, but Grandmama led the rest of them down the cliff path to her terrace, a vast ledge overhanging the bay. The tide was full and tranced in the moonlight, almost inaudibly lapping and swelling far below. A surprise awaited them, a table laid out with plates of lobsters and salads, apricots and wine and iced lemonade. Adriano had brought his wind-up gramophone and for a while they sat and watched the sea and the moving heavens, and listened to a woman's voice in lamentation. "Remember me. Remember me," she pleaded, and Jennifer saw that the clouds and the moon were still and the whole night silenced, attentive only to that desperate cry. Then Jezebel was on her feet, changing the record, winding. "We will dance," she declared. She stretched out her hands to Jennifer's father, but he shook his head and sat back with his shy smile, clasping his glass of wine. Jezebel revolved slowly, furling and whirling her petticoats, staring now at the sea, now at the dark hillside, half angry, half yearning. Jennifer's mother pulled her and Grandmama up. They danced in a circle; their linked hands formed a grave and tender coronal of love. Jennifer forgot everything but this place, wished only to be here forever. Rosa and Adriano were dancing too, very slowly; she could see that Adriano was afraid of colliding with Rosa's huge stomach. Rosa rocked from side to side and Adriano held her at arm's length as though she were some unmanageable agricultural implement. Their shadows all mingled, separated, flowed, pacific as clouds.

And then there were other shadows, an alien blot which spread into the centre of the terrace. Amicia was there, and she was wrapped about a man. At least she had her jacket on again. But the man was Jennifer's father. She saw Amicia's face sagged against his, her red mouth smudging his collar. She saw Adriano gaze wistfully at them and Aunt Rosa looking savagely at Adriano. For a moment as they whirled round she saw her father as she had never seen him, a small man, sly, afraid, and greedy. Then the music stopped, the dance was over. Amicia lurched to the table. The feral cats were scrabbling among the lobsters. "Fucking bloody cats," she yelled. "Disgusting. Where's the music?" No one answered. They all stood still. She saw the gramophone. "Aw, for godsake. Come on, then, I'll give you some music." She grabbed a whole lobster and flung her jacket at the cats. Moving backwards she wrenched at the claws. The wilted orange flower fell out of her hair. She cradled the lobster to her bosom and began to sing, "I can can and you can can, I can can . . ." She kicked her legs up in the air and fell over. The feral cats were on her. She struggled to her feet, kicked a cat, and fell again. She rolled on her back, still singing, rolled onto her side, and went over the edge.

"Time to go home," said Grandmama. They cleared the table into baskets. Jennifer threw Amicia's flower into the sea. It looked quite pretty bobbing there. "Remember me," she thought. She would not. But she would remember the dance. She split a lobster pincer with one crack of her teeth and made her pledge.

DOWN BY THE SEA

Breathing heavily, the Morris Minor toiled over the crest of the coastal ridge. Mary gripped the steering wheel tight, veins bulging on her gnarled old hands, and inched cautiously onto the track ahead, which glittered in frost light, straight as a Roman way far down to the cliff edge; beyond, sea and sky merged, grey into grey. Blanched by winter, the headland grasses stood stiff and motionless. In summer this was a joyous landscape, a profusion of primary colours, crayon-blue sea and azure sky, green cropped turf, scarlet poppies. Where did colour go? Once an emerald moth had balanced, quivering on her bedroom window frame, the purest, deepest translucent green, a platonically perfect green, fading imperceptibly through the days to pallid lettuce. Sorrow, like winter, leaches colour from the world. For a long time after Peter died, Mary moved in a blur of neutral tones, very occasionally offset by a bloody sunset. So it was today, sky and land and sea mournful, hushed, as though waiting for resolution. A storm cloud of lapwings lifted off the headland and darkened the air with omen.

Sidney's house was a garish brightness in the dreary day. He had painted it cornflower blue and it stood defiant on the edge of the high, crumbling cliff. Most of its garden had gone over years ago. Every now and then another yard or two would silently detach and plunge to the shingle sixty feet below. The lower parts of the cliff face had become gelatinous, involved in a mysterious marine process of liquefaction. Soon the house would go too. Sidney was untroubled by this prospect; he believed it would outlive him. Mary doubted this, but she, too, was untroubled. She saw herself floating downwards, like an inverted parasol, an airy scrap of flotsam, to be absumed by elemental wind and water. This was the brink of the world. Nothing but sky and sea, flint stone and the drifting seabirds. Fulmars nested in holes in the upper cliff face; they glided past, their flat faces enigmatic and preoccupied, the tips of their wings almost brushing the grasses. Sidney had called his house the Lobster's Return in anticipation of its watery destiny. Mary imagined the migrant lobsters even now marching in phalanxes over the murky ocean floor, through depths illuminated only by a shafting and fitful sunspot, guided by instinct towards their sunken palace.

Picking her way up the slippery garden path above the grind and groan of sea on shingle, she heard the urgent wails of Sidney's dogs. At once she wished she hadn't come. In the early morning she had been seized by a resentful need for the gardening books she had lent him perhaps four years ago, and had not even thought of since. Vengeful and waspish, she had set forth on a journey which she saw now was pointless. The return of borrowed books was no longer a matter of principle to her; nor was she, or Sidney, come to that, likely now to be planting any of those shrubs, bulbs, perennials, middle- or back-of-the-border subjects. *Heuchera* "Stormy Seas," heliotrope, mulberry, quince, or medlar; *Rosa mundi* "Versicolor," "Belle de Crécy," the strangely named masculine roses, "Parkdirektor Riggers," "Rambling Rector," or "Robert le Diable," whom she had brought once as a gift for Sidney because it resembled him: "procumbent in habit with a vinous flush." The litany had lost its power to move her; those days were gone and her garden could go with them. How long before it reverted to bramble and nettle and wilderness, seeding grasses, dandelions, thistledown? Before Sidney's house went under the sea? Before her own demise?

She pushed the front door open. "Come up to the drawing room," cried Sidney from above. Warily she skirted the kitchen; it was worse than last time, with even more bread. Every flat surface was a litter of mouldering slices, crumpets lurid with verdigris, tureens and platters overspilling pockmarked loaves, carbonised toast, rolls turned to rock. She had asked him why he didn't throw it all out. "I'm keeping it for the peacocks," he said absently. The last peacock was long dead and the peacocks' tamarisk walk lay under water now. She pointed this out. "Well, the birds, then."

But not even Sidney could wreck the drawing room. Three tall bay windows overhung the sea, and on the walls between, great mirrors drew in the light so that at sunset the room was a spinning vortex of pink and gold and azure, and then a phoenix's nest of molten fire. In the cold gaze of this February morning a shift of clouds suggested changing weather, soothed her, confirmed the mutability of all things. Who should care about the bread and the birds?

Sidney hadn't done much about getting dressed. In his floor-length red brocade dressing gown he tottered about the room looking for sherry glasses and wheezing. Mary declined the sherry and he ignored her. Dog hairs clung around the rim of her glass. She placed it on the nearest small table, one of a sequence which stood in inconvenient positions across the room, bearing tiny troops drawn up in battle formation, rearguards, vanguards, pincer movements, cavalry and infantry and artillery; awaiting their high command. "Is it still Waterloo?" she asked politely. "Absolutely not. Oudenarde. If the dogs don't get in we could have victory by nightfall. And then I'm moving on to Malplaquet. What larks!" he said, rubbing his hands together. God, thought Mary. Five minutes more of this and she could go. There was precious little likelihood of victory by nightfall. The dogs had two purposes. One was to gallop about the headland, terrorising ramblers; then they would collapse and sleep noisily in the back kitchen. But, when bored, they would work their door latch loose and come crashing up the stairs. Well, one of them crashed; the other scrabbled. Both were spoilers of the fortunes of war. With one mighty swing of her tail, the Newfoundland despatched battalions piecemeal about the room; the Pekinese pounced among the fallen, snuffling and dismembering. Sidney would be lying helpless and breathless in his armchair, toppled by the Newfoundland's ecstatic greeting, high leap of embrace, fervent licks and jocular toss of the head. Stalactites of slobber slouched shining down the walls. When he had caught his breath, Sidney would make his joke. "O, my America," he gasped, "my Newfoundland." He had called the dog America for this purpose. The Peke was called Frean after Peek Freans, a biscuit firm which had long ceased to trade, so that no one was amused. Not that they would have been anyhow; and according to Sidney only two people had ever recognised the America allusion. He used it as an intellectual benchmark, he claimed, exonerating Mary's failure to respond by saying that in her very distant youth no girl would have been allowed to read a poem so shocking. Actually, Mary thought, he was even older than she was; and the close of girlhood did not signal an end to poetry reading. She intended now to leave before this all happened again.

As she drove down the coast road to Cromer, she realised that she had left all the books behind. She left the Morris tucked into the taxi rank by the church and hobbled through the great oak door. Bonily she settled into a hard, polished pew. She was tired and jangled. But then the familiar, enfolding peace came upon her, conferred by high windows of sea water glass, through which she could just discern the shadow forms of pigeons tumbling from the tower. *A pigeon tumbling in clear summer air, a laughing schoolboy without grief or care*. She remembered that summer feeling from childhood, running with arms outflung through the silver birches, head back, eyes dazzled, almost flying. To swoop, to soar; all things then were possible. She closed her eyes and slept and dreamed of white feathers falling like winter round her.

Meanwhile Sidney, snugly wrapped against the cold, sits out on the cliff edge and stares at his soldiers. They lie in a heap of disorder on a folding table which is topped by an artful tray depicting Balmoral. He can think of nothing to do with them. Far below the sea prowls and sloughs over the shingle; the tide is full and the noise of sucking and disgorging drowns out the shrill yaps of the Pekinese and the baritone boom of the Newfoundland as they race about the headland, drowns out the working of Sidney's brain. He sips a gin and tonic and chews his lower lip. He gathers his coats and dressing gown about him; the late afternoon chill intensifies and the sky, which for an hour had been a tender blue, a fickle promise of spring, has whitened. Time to go in, he thinks, heaving himself up. But it is already too late; the turf beneath his feet buckles and wrenches and slithers forward and downward. Sidney and his soldiers are gone, pitched in a headlong welter of earth and rock and sand and startled birds whose wingtips buffet him as he hurtles into darkness.

The dogs have noticed nothing, but after a comfortless night, tomorrow at low tide they will retrieve some of the soldiers and chew them up. Small children will find more and take them home in pockets clammy with sand and shells, dead crabs and starfish; but no one will find Sidney for a long time. He has been rolled far out on a riptide, and will emerge, eyeless and shrouded in bladderwrack, one bright summer morning, miles down the coast on a Blue Flag beach, forever blighting the lives of a pair of ramblers.

MISSING

"*C'est un beau chien*," said the Frenchman. Mary and he stared at the black lurcher curvetting and galloping in and out and round about the vast cylindrical straw bales, zigzagging almost horizontal to the stubble.

"She's a bitch," said Mary. "Actually," she added, so as not to seem rude, although she felt like being rude. Why was he here at all, when he was her daughter's friend? And why wasn't Ellen here?

"*Chienne alors*," shrugged the Frenchman, "*même chose*."

Rage mounted in Mary.

"It's not at all the same thing; perhaps it is in France. Here we look differently at dogs."

Wood pigeons cooed and mourned in the heavy August trees, tarnished already with the ebbing days of summer. An exhaust backfired, scattering the pigeons out against the clouded sky. Ellen's car jolted up the drive, roaring and revving. A Cromer Carni-

191

val pennant clung to the wireless aerial and two huge grizzled dogs glowered from the windows. Thank God for that, thought Mary. Now perhaps he'll go. In the sharp shadow cast by the bales he looked like Louis Jourdan playing Dracula. Or the man on the old Gitanes packet. Or was it Gauloises? She was too old for all this. Now Ellen stood beside him in her dreadful paramilitary trousers, and they were beaming at her. Extraordinary behaviour. The low sun dazzled her eyes.

"We've something to tell you, Mother," said Ellen. The Frenchman nodded vigorously.

"You say," he urged.

"No, you." Ellen pushed him forward.

Mary's heart lurched. Surely they weren't planning to marry. Not *Ellen*.

He cleared his throat.

"I have found the grave," he pronounced, each word slow and careful. "I have found at last the grave of your husband."

Ellen's mother, Mary, had learned a few things in her time, as she sometimes told her unfriendly daughter. One of these was to live with grief, or rather to live without it, beyond it. She had been alone a long time now, existing, Ellen thought, not only beyond grief, but also beyond love. Mary's husband had died invisibly in the Normandy landings, missing, presumed dead, a couple of months before Ellen was born. These days Mary didn't think about him much. Sometimes, but not often. And she had never thought much about Ellen. She was old and dusty and almost immaterial, shrinking her way out of life. She tried to live in abeyance from mortality. She preferred the evanescent, brooding endlessly on wind and weather, hunched over her wireless. If she considered life or death she became weighed down, oppressed: there had been too much of both and she could not succumb to either. The passing moment exacted all the strength she had left. "I'm tired of living and I'm tired of dying," she sang to herself. That wasn't right and she couldn't remember any of the other lines and she didn't care. Words came uninvited and tangled in her brain and set themselves to music. They would hang about for weeks, until they were re-placed by something else, a phrase or two of poetry, an advertising slogan, some old-time ribaldry.

Even on this strange evening, when Ellen and the Frenchman had gone, and dusk and owls had invaded her garden, her skull was buzzing with a sprightly jingle:

It's a fine tanking day
   And as balmy as May

And the crew to the tank parks have hurried.

She persuaded herself there was nothing she could do about it, and it was better than thinking, when there was time to pass before any hope of sleep. So, humming briskly, she moved her frail body about her house; her bones clicked and creaked like knitting needles. The air was cold now, so cold that she sipped it, rather than breathed it in, a chill presaging the bleak East Anglian winter. Draughts skittered through the window frames and lifted the edges of threadbare rugs. As darkness gathered through those unlit, unpeopled rooms, she could almost believe that she had attained the ghostly state of her aspiration. There but not there. Intimations of the past lay all about her and in her solitude she might choose to remember, to forget, or to rearrange. Only very rarely, as now, was she caught unawares, overwhelmed by a great, retching pang of agonised grief, which left her shaken and gasping, clutching at the walls for support, slithering to the floor.

She sat there very still and stared at the runnels on her fingertips, where dust and skin cells merged, ashes to ashes. An old familiar image lingered in her head, a heave of sea the colour of muddy milk, waves racing and breaking under a dingy sky, frameless, boundless, implacable. And with it a sense of absolute terror. Slowly it receded. She breathed more steadily and concentrated on her becalming method, a memory of a house from her Norfolk childhood, the home of her cousins. It was damp and half derelict, and when they had got round to making it habitable, after many years of habitation, a slab of rotten plaster had crumbled from the wall, revealing a staring, ecstatic eye, a web of golden hair. Soon a colonnade of saints and heavenly bodies gazed out in troubled piety from the dining room walls.

"All the way round too," grumbled Uncle Randal. "What on earth are we to do?" The planned rewiring would cause grievous injuries. The mighty, smoking fire would discolour and desiccate. Worse was to come. In the upstairs corridors and largest bedroom an ancient hunting scene emerged, all swishing tails and stabbing fangs and spears. A boar at bay snarled and a crown rolled beneath the stamp of hooves, just where the socket for Aunt Ruth's electric fire should be.

"Wheesht," said Randal. "Aye, *wheesht*'s the word," agreed the workmen. Within days the figures were again immured, sealed in by thick layers of plaster and distemper. As a nervous small child, Mary had found the thought of those saints and horsemen, vigilant but invisible, wonderfully comforting. Now she imagined herself joining them, becoming part of that house, fading slowly into the plaster, into self-effacement, there and not there. Thus fortified she accomplished without effort the three-hot-water-bottle evening ritual and retired to bed.

But this night was different. Peter has been found. Or, more likely, bits of Peter. She thought again of that muddy sea, breaking forever on its forlorn strand. She had gone to that great curve of beach once, years ago, with her friend Josephine, trying to imagine what Peter had seen, last seen before he fell. Josephine had said it would be good for her, a laying of a ghost. Mary didn't find it good at all. Josephine had brought a picnic to enjoy at this maritime charnel house. Mary walked down to the sea; the tide was far out and the sands shone under a pallid, fitful sun.

She was remembering the first time she met Peter. He was dressed in cricket whites, waiting to bat. He leaned slightly forward on his bat and she saw a crusader leaning on his sheathed sword. A perfect, gentle knight in a world then crowded with possibility, a future in which the past would renew itself, complementing and deepening the present; no opportunity would ever be cancelled, no prospect rendered void. One would grow a little older, but not to any irretrievable degree. There had been a day in Oxford when they had wandered together through water meadows thronged with cow parsley and birdsong. Mary was intensely happy. So many years later, how well she recalled that day. It was warm and uncertain; spring sunlight glanced through rain-soaked leaves and the air was blurred and pungent with blossom and earth and damp, charged with an erotic excitement and poignancy which Mary had noticed then and since in ancient university cities. An exhalation compounded of hundreds of yearning springtimes, aspiration thwarted, unfocused desire, urgent joy and mild, pastoral melancholy. She felt a quiver of fear.

"You want to watch this place," she said. "It's an ambush, isn't it? Toils of enchantment. Toil and moil, warp and weft. Funny that; could you say it warps you?" She eyed Peter sidelong, hoping to provoke him. But he wasn't listening; or rather he was listening to the bells, clamorous as always, and the cuckoo calling over the high walls. Spring-struck, he moved, tranced as a pilgrim through the scent of wallflowers and then of bluebells as they turned into woodland along the river. A path, freshly hacked through undergrowth, led them to a clearing, and in the centre of the clearing a scowling priapic statue squatted, one arm extended as if grudgingly to shake hands. As they drew closer they saw that in fact the arm was pointing them back towards the river. Beyond stretched an overgrown garden, starred pink with campion and bramble. The sun shone strongly now and insects hummed and buzzed through the tall flowering grasses, nettles, and elder. The house at the top of the garden was smothered in creeper; vine and clematis clambered to the roof edge, felt their way under the tiles, still dark from the early rain, and curved luxuriantly down again. They had wrenched the balconies from the wall and suspended them in airy cages of leaf and tendril. Above the porch an odd rectangle of brickwork remained bare, shadowed randomly by the faintest of markings, like ancient drawings or a forgotten script.

"Look," said Peter, "just watch this." The markings were gaining in definition; they resolved into imposing Roman capitals, they grouped, they formed a word: PARADISE, they proclaimed. Mary sat down abruptly in the sodden grass. She was frightened and hot and something had bitten her on the eyelid. Her heart thudded. Peter was smiling down at her.

"It's all right," he said, "don't look like that. It's meant to be a surprise. And I didn't know if it would really happen."

"What on earth do you mean? How did you know? Have you been here before? What is it *doing*?"

Peter pulled her up and hugged her. "It's lichens."

Lichens. Mary had never heard this word pronounced. *Lichens.* She was overwhelmed with love for him.

"This place used to be a pub or an inn or something and it had metal letters on the wall. You get these lichens left underneath them and they develop just for a few minutes when it's hot after it's been raining. Then they fade away again. Wait and see."

Mary could not bear to watch the fading.

"Let's go, quick, and then it'll always be there."

It was too late; the space was blank again and an ancient, angry face glared down from an upstairs window. Squashed and distorted against the pane, its bulging cheeks resembled the gargoyle features in the clearing.

So it had been.

———

She became aware now of the chill of the sands; she was shivering. She glanced back at the picnicking Josephine and could only make out a huddled form, intent on its Tupperware boxes. The shore and the dunes and the further cliff line were blanked out by a low-hanging thick white fog. Looming here and there near the waterline, the tractors which dragged speedboats down to the sea might have been the rusty skeletons of tanks, and occasional distant figures were visible only in parts, a head, a glimpse of torso, a flailing arm. The tide crept swiftly inshore, the colour of her imagining, muddy milk. Fear gathered, thudding, in her head and heart.

———

So on that cold August night, Mary lay awake; she thought of Peter and his grave and all the half-life lived since he had gone, the surprising resolution of middle age into old age and her relief then that soon it would all be over. And her guilt now at so many years wasted, that others could have cherished. But if Peter had not been taken from her, how different it would have been. She might have loved Ellen, instead of finding her a dismal encumbrance. Ellen might have grown up to be pretty and loving and marriageable in-stead of going around in army surplus clothes and breeding weird curly coated dogs with webbed feet.

"As mentioned in Shakespeare. *Water rugs*," she claimed.

Everything that had mattered was so long ago; she thought her feelings had all leached away and she had nothing left. Nothing but that intermittent pain of missing Peter, of missing being loved, of the abiding loss of her share of the world.

All that summer a comet had hung in the sky above Mary's garden. Ellen claimed that it was also suspended above the shan-tytown ensemble of wire-netting pens and corrugated-iron huts which comprised her kennels, but Mary had certainly not seen it there. She enjoyed the comet's strangeness, its air of preoccupation, as if it were brooding upon its imminent departure into unreach-able black voids for another four thousand years. She felt person-ally privileged by its coming and she treasured its unmatchable evanescence; it made her bold and dismissive and untruthful.

"What then is life?" she asked it. She was seized by an irratio-nal fear that it would disappear while she and Ellen were in France at Peter's grave. The night before they left she stood out on her dewy lawn, hands clasped tight; staring up at it, she recited silently a rhyme half forgotten from childhood:

Star light, star bright
First star I see tonight
I wish I may, I wish I might
Have the wish I wish this night.

But she didn't know what to wish. The comet dreamed on, impervious. Somewhere across the river a goose was laughing.

———————

They drove to Portsmouth in Ellen's rackety, dog-smelling car. Tufts of fur eddied down shafts of sunlight and strewed themselves delicately over the padded shoulders of Mary's severe grey coat and skirt, still very serviceable after fifty years of wardrobe and mothballs. On the boat, out on deck and hanging on to the rail, she shut her eyes and tried to will herself to push through time and emerge on the far side, a forties sweetheart, a forces sweetheart, Peter's sweetheart. But her legs were too wobbly and her hands too gnarled. The bright breeze made her cheekbones ache; her eyes watered.

Ellen had rented a house near Caen. It was unnecessarily large, and gloomy; on the walls were tattered, blackened copies of ancient funeral notices, and Ellen announced proudly that it was here that Charlotte Corday had stayed in the weeks before she murdered Marat.

"It's dead cheap because of that," she said.

But it had a large and beautiful garden where apples hung red and gold from trees swagged with mistletoe. At night shooting stars plunged from the heavens, but Mary looked in vain for the comet.

On a brilliant blue day of Indian summer, Ellen took Mary to the graveyard. Slow and silent, they walked together up the long green slope between the crowding multitude of white stones.

Mary leaned heavily on Ellen's arm; she had no thoughts at all, no feelings, only a thudding heart and a great weariness. But as they turned down the avenue of Peter's grave her step quickened. She let go of Ellen's arm; she pushed her hair back and smoothed it, she shook out her skirt and moved forward, head high, serene and eager, a ghostly bride advancing to her lover.

In late afternoon they returned to the house. Ellen's friend François brought tea out to the garden. Mary took her cup and smiled at him, surprising him.

"Thank you, Peter darling," she said, surprising him more. She studied her tea, its swaying disc of surface. It was reminding her of something, but she could not focus on it; she saw a pinpoint of sunlight reflected and she heard the roaring of the sea. She slipped sideways from her chair to the grass and lay there, staring unseeing up at François, her hands still clasping the delicate cup.

———————

They cremated her in Caen and Ellen took the ashes, a rosebush, and a trowel back to the war graves. She laid the ashes in Peter's oblong of turf and above she planted the rose. She walked away down the green slope to the gateway. Poppies trembled there in the long grass and she thought how strange it was that they should be the flowers of remembrance and of forgetfulness. She believed then, and not for the first time, that she had inherited her mother's cold, passionless nature, for she felt nothing but a powerful longing to be done with all this, and never to return. Several days later she found beneath a carpet in Mary's house a dusty brown paper bag.

In it was a photograph of her parents as she had never seen them, he in his uniform, she in a flowered dress, laughing and young and ardent, gazing at each other.

"Before my time," Ellen thought. Out in the twilight sky, the comet was tilting away into renewed aeons of solitude. She was overwhelmed by desolation, a longing to arrest the moment, to declare that love is as strong as death; but this she could not do. Anyhow, it was time to feed her dogs.

CARBORUNDUM

She was perfecting her wintry smile in a hand mirror tarnished with verdigris. The face that looked back at her was white as snow, or chalk rather, her own powdery chalk. When she ran her hands down her cheeks, smoothing away the excess, it settled in a fine dust over her shoulders. The wind whisked long hanks of grizzled hair across her eyes and a cold sun dazzled her. She reached beneath the tarpaulin and withdrew her mother's old magenta jumper. It was shrunken now and felted with the years of damp and dews, but it provided just enough protection for this November afternoon. Carefully she lowered her legs over the edge of the platform and began the slow descent, breathing a little heavily now as the soles of her boots tested, then found purchase on the slippery ladder rungs. As always, she felt a flicker of relief when she reached the carpet of beechnut husks and sodden leaves.

She dragged the high old pram out of the shed and set forth

along the cliff track, gripping the handle tightly, bent against the wind. Beneath, the sea prowled back and forth, complaining.

When she trudged along like this, she was able to think, or, more important, remember. Up in her trees she was too busy; life hung on a concatenation of infinitely laborious small tasks, and as she grew older, everything took longer. This was how she wanted it to be. She was eking out existence, waiting to go. For others all things might be passing, but for her all things long since had passed. And the fact that she generally remembered the same things did not trouble her. For so long things had been the same, two separate samenesses, one more detailed than the other. Thirty years rotting away with Mother, thirty years in the trees. Was there a story at all, a shape? Is there ever?

The lofty rocking motion of the ancient perambulator had perhaps been a foreshadow of the swaying beech tree branches, systole and diastole of wind and weather, the rhythms of her world; for as an infant she had occupied this very vehicle, propped on lace-edged pillows of cambric, propelled back and forth by adoring relatives. Who had all died. Except, of course, for Mother, who had died later, far too late and who had certainly not adored her. Even now, the thought of her mother made her knuckles strain white under their carapace of rough red skin, brown blotches, veins serpentine and glaucous. "Won't you ever take pride in your appearance, Marjory?" demanded a ghostly voice. "Look at your hands. Anyone would think you were a skivvy." Her heart then had cried out in silence that she was indeed a skivvy, enslaved by a cold and cruel despot who had tricked her into servitude and would not ever release her.

The summer when she had finished boarding school and was about to go to university she had found herself consumed by a great weariness, headaches, and shooting pains, so that she could scarcely get out of bed, could not eat, could not speak. The doctor said she had brain fever and she must rest for a long time or it would not go away. How Mother's eyes shone; she was sharpening her knives. "Just you stay in bed, darling, and I'll look after you. It will be fun to have you properly at home after all these years I've been on my own. While *you've* been off being *educated*," she added with a tinkly laugh. "And what an expense that was," she said a few weeks later. "Really, I have to say I'm quite glad that university is out of the question now." "Only for this year, surely?" mumbled an alarmed Marjory, capable now of speech, less capable of enduring interminable afternoons by the unlit drawing room fire, gazing out at the merge of pale sea and pale sky. "Time will tell," said Mother, her eyes no longer bright but dull and critical. "Certainly you won't be going anywhere at all unless you put on some weight." How could anyone gain weight on a diet of calves' foot jelly and tripe, borne grudgingly on trays to her room? She was forbidden to eat downstairs; she realised that this was because Mother was eating normal food and would find her company and the sight of her not eating her invalid food unbearably irritating.

So began the sequestration, the erosion of possibility and aspiration, stretching into years, into forever. For when at last Marjory was well again, Mother chose to retire to her bed, suffering from some unidentifiable malaise. "Perhaps I've caught that nasty disease off you, after all that time nursing you. Dr. Fox is baffled, of course. So lucky for me that you're here, darling." This was the second time in two years that she had called Marjory darling.

As she reached the outskirts of the village, a shower of pebbles skittered against the pram wheels and ricocheted off, stinging into her ankles. She stopped stock-still and turned her chalky face towards the jeering children; slowly, deliberately, she smiled her frozen smile, her eyes expressionless. The children melted into the dunes and marram grass. The village shop smelt of paraffin and apples as it always had done, and no one flinched at her appearance. They packed her box up as usual, and it was only after she had laboured out with it to the pram, refusing offers of help, and had moved into her return journey that one rolled eyes at another, heads were shaken, voices lowered. Just for a moment; there were more interesting topics with novelty value, winter holiday tenants, the tideline of wreckage left by the half-term break, the occupants of the bus shelter. Marjory plodded on, up to the clifftop path and the stir of the wind. Already the light was fading and the bleached grasses shivered; the sea was ruffled, metallic grey in the chill of evening. An occasional poppy still trembled on the dunes' edge and as the path climbed she could distinguish the small pale stars of chamomile, but colour was leaching from the landscape, into a dying winter world. She looked back at the lit windows of the village and was unmoved. Once she would have envied the lives she imagined in those lamplit rooms, familial meals, exchange of the day's events, a loving kindness reserved for those within, implicit in the shrug and glide of curtains drawn against the outsider. Exclusion was now her natural state; no doubt it always had been, but then she had not recognised it, then when she still had small hopes of a normal life and believed what people said.

The summer Mother had gone, there had been a song blaring endlessly from the wireless in the shop and from people's cars; most of the words were unintelligible to her, but there was a single-line refrain, "The day the music died." That was the summer when one life had ended and another begun, the day his letter had come and the wedding was off, the dining room full of presents which she would never use, the accoutrements of a real house, an un-discovered place waiting to be realised. The wedding dress in its shrouds of tissue swayed and twisted in the draught from her bed-room window; it watched her, the faceless ghost of her trusting self; and she thought it mocked her. "How could you think you could ever be a bride?" it whispered. "Be loved and cherished and make golden perfect toast in the toaster, wake to the welcome of the Goblin Teasmaid, iron crisp, fragrant linen on that pristine padded ironing board. Share your life in the warmth while the sea wind batters the windows." There might have been a dog, and cat, even a child. All gone that day, the day the music died, the day she took to the trees.

She stood on the cliff edge, where you could see nothing but sea and sky and the curved rim of the horizon, and heard the hushed roar of water ceaselessly shifting stones. All things were temporal and passing; the cliff itself, perilously layered, would slither someday soon into the heave of ocean, and the white birds floating beneath her now, untroubled, would find themselves new sanctuaries on the raw exposed rock face. Turning away, she was aware of sharp pain in her hips and in her knees where her old bones scraped and ground each other into rough jagging surfaces. The stones were better served by the sea; it left them smooth and shining. Cliff and sea, hip and knee; a cheerless little grindstone song. Near to shore on a post, a cormorant was drying his outspread wings, densely black and cruciform against the swelling tide.

At the back gate she glanced into the letterbox. Nothing but snails. Beyond the parched winter grasses and shrivelled stands of dock leaves the house loomed, blinded by shutters. Sometimes she played with the notion of going in there; sometimes she crept around it like a thief, peering through cracks in the shutters and cobwebs at vistas and sepia rooms lined with bookcases, heavy mahogany tables, grimly upholstered armchairs. But when she saw the wedding presents still there in the dining room, and when she thought of the dress performing its twirling dance upstairs, her heart would thump and she would begin to shake.

That night, in the tree house, her eagle home, she could not sleep for the pain in her hips. Each morning she would wake colder and stiffer. In the light of day she knew the rooks were watching her. It was too late now for it to matter where or whether she lived or died. This pain and cold would also pass. All those years of falling leaves and rooks nesting and spring's return, distant foghorns, drownings and foundering ships, wind and weather, had purged her, bleached her like driftwood. She was memory now, nothing more nor less. One day, maybe this day, in a flurry of shining leaves and eyes and beaks she would have gone and then the rooks would have her. So let it be; her story was over.

IN THE CAGE

It was April, but it might have been midwinter, so wan and chill the sky. The few green leaves were dank and sullen; the new season was suspended, confounded in ancient cold, cold in your bones, cold, cold, my girl. On such a day there is nothing to lift the spirits, earth and air and sea spellbound and hushed in this cruel aftermath, the blackthorn winter.

As she drove down the narrow track through the heath she was utterly consumed by the bleak world, its only brightness shed by the snow light of the blackthorn blossom and the lurid yellow gorse. Beneath, the church and its tower, moored on their ridge above the marshes, were a discordant note, a looming lonely statement of human will and aspiration. She believed she had no time for such things today, or ever, come to that, locked in her carapace of misery, her face a wilfully downturned mask, her heart a stone. So now she was surprised to find herself seated stiff and upright in a pew, her hands knotted together, not in prayer but in a desperate unfocused anxiety which she wanted God to resolve. Inside her head black shapes and words collided and reformed and repeated themselves. While she yearned for some sort of absolution, she did not believe she could find it.

————

She had thought the church empty, but a woman was moving down the aisle towards her, also wringing her hands. "There's a bird in here," she said, and a tear rolled down her cheek. "Poor thing, just look at it." It was hurling itself over and over at the high window, its wings pattering on the glass; then it dipped out of sight, then it was back. Now it flew lower, resting for moments on the deep sill. So small a bird, a drab little brown thing. "It's a nightingale," the woman said. "All the way from Africa, to be trapped in here. It should be up on the heath, singing."

"It's not trapped, really," she told the woman. "Look, the doors are wide open; it will find its way out." How she wanted the woman gone, and the bird too; she had a great longing for sleep and she closed her eyes. In her own darkness and against her will she kept thinking about the bird. A nightingale. She had never heard one, let alone seen one. She imagined its journey over deserts, over seas, a mere speck of a creature flung about in winds, drenched with rain, baffled by sudden sunlight, its wings beating resolutely onward, until, perhaps using the tower as a landmark, it floated inland high above the church to its breeding ground in the dense thickets of the heath. If freedom is the knowledge of necessity, there in those twisted branches of gorse and blackthorn the bird was free and its song was a song of triumph. It had achieved its necessary purpose, and its eye was bright with it.

Not so this poor lost creature, bewildered, perhaps even stunned, for now the church was silent. The woman must have gone. And maybe the bird was gone too.

Gradually the familiar peace enfolded her, drifting down like early dusk among the pillars which reared like trees, beneath the windows whose glass was the colour of sea water. She might have slept, lulled by that sense of sanctuary, but then she was thinking again of the bird and how her sanctuary was its prison. She opened her eyes. The bird was there, motionless, perched on the end of the pew. She could not breathe. In a moment she had it clasped in her cupped hands. Through her fingers she could see it, quite passive; she felt the pulsing of its tiny heart and its warm folded wings. She remembered the childhood rhyme for hands so clasped: This is the church and there is the steeple; open the doors and out come the people. Solemn and purposeful, she stepped over the threshold bearing before her the delicate burden, now become a sacred trust.

She was happy here, free and light. Her world held nothing but herself and the bird. They were out in the churchyard, under the eye of heaven, and she flung her arms high in the exultant gesture she had seen in statues of the Virgin, declaring her baby to God and man and the universe. The nightingale would leap from her spread palms into the wide air, falter for a moment, and then be speeding to its destiny. And life would go on and there would be a time for song. But although her hands lay flat and open as an altar under the sky the bird did not move; it was on its side, its eye glazed; its beak had opened in a soundless cry.

She found a stick. With cold, stiff fingers she scraped a shallow grave among the other graves. She was not sad yet: perhaps later she would be. She had an odd sense that she had done what she had come to do, and now she could turn homewards. It started to rain and just as suddenly stopped. Wet leaves glistened in pale sunlight. At the top of the hill three hooded figures emerged from the scrubland and waved her down. "It's the nightingales," they said. "Turn off your engine, just for a moment." All the air was filled with a whirling confusion of whistles and chirrups but then she distinguished the long notes of piercing sweetness, the cadences, trills, and occasional weird gutturals. She glanced for confirmation at the hooded ones and they nodded. For a little while yet purged of self, she listened and she thought of the dead and the small bird with them down in the graveyard between the sound of nightingales and the sigh of the sea, and the world revolving slowly on its axis into hope. The beauty of sound issuing from invisible creatures in impenetrable undergrowth, thorns and twisted branches, reminded her of Leonardo's remark that art breathes in containment and is suffocated by freedom. She wondered if Leonardo ever knew a nightingale.

ABOUT THE AUTHORS

Elspeth Barker (1940–2022) wrote and published her first and only novel, *O Caledonia*, at the age of fifty-one. It was awarded the Winifred Holtby Memorial Prize and was shortlisted for the Whitbread Prize. In her career as a journalist, Elspeth wrote for *The Independent*, *The Observer*, *The Sunday Times*, *London Review of Books*, and others. For ten years in the 1980s Elspeth taught Latin at what she describes as a naughty girls' school on the Norfolk coast. Later, she worked as a lecturer in creative writing at the Norwich University of the Arts. She was married to the poet George Barker, with whom she had five children; they lived in rural Norfolk. After his death in 1991, she lived on there with numerous badly behaved animals and a home that welcomed everyone.

Raffaella Barker has been writing novels since the age of twenty-six, and has been a promiscuous reader all her life. She has written nine novels and worked as a journalist for *Country Life*, *The Sunday Times*, *Condé Nast Traveller*, and *Harper's Bazaar*. Raffaella lectured in the Creative Writing programme at the University of East Anglia, and continues to teach creative writing privately. The eldest of Elspeth and George Barker's five children, she has inherited their penchant for badly behaved animals and, about her home on the north Norfolk coast, has said, "The Norfolk landscape sends a shiver through my soul."